WHERE TO BELONG

T0347915

Victor Esses

WHERE TO BELONG

OBERON BOOKS
LONDON

WWW.OBERONBOOKS.COM

First published in 2019 by Oberon Books Ltd

521 Caledonian Road, London N7 9RH

Tel: +44 (0) 20 7607 3637 / Fax: +44 (0) 20 7607 3629

e-mail: info@oberonbooks.com

www.oberonbooks.com

PB ISBN: 9781786827982

E ISBN: 9781786827999

Cover image © Yorgos Petrou

Inside images © Alex Brenner

eBook conversion by Lapiz Digital Services, India.

Visit www.oberonbooks.com to read more about all our books and to buy them. You will also find features, author interviews and news of any author events, and you can sign up for e-newsletters so that you're always first to hear about our new releases.

Victor Esses is an associate artist to CASA Festival. He has been associate director to maverick international director Gerald Thomas.

Performance/maker credits include: *Unfamiliar* (CASA, Arcola Theatre); *Sound of Us* (Tallinn Larp Festival, The Smoke at Theatre Deli); *Dis Place* (Camden People's Theatre, Arts Admin, The Glory, Latitude Festival); *Codependently Yours* (Arcola Theatre Lab, VFD, Albany Theatre).

Directing includes: *Venus Flytrap* (Theatre 503, performed by Jonny Woo); *Tapped Out!* (Tristan Bates); *The Assault* (Old Red Lion); *Repast 2* (Theatre 503); *The Last Days of Gilda* (Arcola Theatre).

Performing includes: *Tunguska Event – History Marches on a Table* (Whitechapel Gallery); *Faraway, So Close* (Old Fire Station); *Trojan Horse/Rainbow Flag* (film by Ian Giles).

For more information, visit **www.victoresses.com**
@vhesses (Twitter)
@victoresses (Instagram)

Where to Belong was scratched at CASA Festival, Southwark Playhouse, London on 14 October 2017. It opened at Rich Mix, London on 19 January 2018. It was performed as part of VOILA! Festival at The Cockpit, London on 13 and 16 November 2018, and on 31 July–25 August 2019 at Summerhall, Edinburgh. Shortlisted for the Emerge Performance Prize; in association with CASA and Rich Mix.

Written, conceived and performed by Victor Esses

Set, costume and projections by Yorgos Petrou

Lighting design by David Doyle (Edinburgh)
and Pablo Fernandez Baz

Assistant Director Fernanda De Moura

Stage Manager Lucy Morris (Edinburgh)
and Fernanda De Moura

Production Manager (Edinburgh) Jack Greenyer
for Infinity Technical Services

Produced by Ellie Keel for Ellie Keel Productions,
with Jennifer Lunn (Associate Producer) and
Gabrielle Leadbeater (Production and
Marketing Associate)

Ellie Keel CASA RICH MIX
PRODUCTIONS

Special thanks to the following individuals and organizations for making the show possible:

Daniel Goldman, Cordelia Grierson and the whole CASA Festival team

Oliver Carruthers, Josh McNorton, Martha Rumney, Natasha Clark and all at Rich Mix

Sharlit Deyzac, Amy Clare Tasker, Dave Wybrow and the whole VOILA! and Cockpit crews

Verity Leigh, Tom Forster and all at Summerhall

Serena Grasso and Oberon Books

Everyone who worked on *Where to Belong*, including Mira Yonder, Mariana Aristizábal Pardo and Katie Melton

Phoebe Boswell, Bryony Kimmings, Frederica Boswell, Juan Ayala, Gaël Le Cornec, Fernanda Mandagará, Jairo Bouer and Bahi Ghubril

Everyone who has attended sharings, rehearsals and performances of the piece.

An extra special thank you to Jihad Hashim and Waleed Jarjouhi for giving the last push needed for Victor to make the trip to Lebanon, and for welcoming him and supporting him in his journey.

Introduction

Victor told me about *Where to Belong* a good year or so before he invited me to watch a run-through in his small studio space in an office building. I'd seen various iterations of *Codependently Yours* so I thought I had a sense of what I might be about to see...

And then Victor started. A different voice emerged; a calmness, a certainty and an assurance of purpose I hadn't seen before in Victor's work. It felt like an artist finding their voice after a long hard journey deep within themselves. I programmed it to be performed at CASA immediately.

I am tempted to say that Victor bares his soul in this play, but I think that it would be more accurate to say that Victor bares his flesh. To tell his story, Victor sheds his skin and invites us to shed ours. It is a piece and performance which chips away at the boundaries we put up between ourselves. Through the course of the hour we spend together, the borders between Victor and the audience dissolve – we go from listening to Victor's story to helping him tell it; we are invited to share who we would save; ultimately, we are invited onto the stage where our bodies literally, physically meet Victor's and Victor's body meets ours. *Where to Belong* is here and now: infinitely, impossibly close to the people we love and who love us. It is, I think, a performance without membrane. It is, I think, a remarkable achievement.

I love this piece, I'm delighted that it continues to be performed, and I'm delighted to see it in print. I hope it proves to be as much of a balm to you and your heart as it has been to me and mine.

Daniel Goldman
Founding Artistic Director,
CASA Theatre Festival

Dedicated to Yorgos. To Jay. And to everyone
who has ever struggled with a sense of belonging.

The performance space consists of moving boxes, a little pink table with a laptop on top, a green-grass rug centre stage, a microphone on a stand, a straw chair with a cassette tape recorder on top, another small box with a mini-projector on top. Cables.

The audience enter the space. VICTOR welcomes them. He asks one person to follow him. In a quiet corner, he records a question and the person's answer into a cassette tape recorder. He thanks them and gets another person. He asks about five.

VICTOR:

What makes a home for you?

Audience member replies.

What does belonging mean to you?

Audience member replies.

Do you feel you belong here? Now?

Audience member replies.

Can you think of a significant memory from your childhood that represents home?

Audience member replies.

Where is home for you?

Audience member replies.

Can you think of a song that reminds you of home? Could you sing it?

Audience member replies. VICTOR goes to the microphone.

I'm feeling… *(VICTOR says how he is feeling.)*

He walks up to a member of the audience.

How are you feeling?

Audience member replies.

VICTOR asks a couple more audience members.

*

VICTOR looks up at the STAGE MANAGER.

Are we ready *(name of STAGE MANAGER)*?

STAGE MANAGER replies. When the STAGE MANAGER clears it, VICTOR takes his slippers off.

Good, so I can get on with the intro, or prologue, or whatever you want to call it.

VICTOR walks centre stage.

Prologue

VICTOR:

How do I place my body in this space?

My white body.

My Jewish body.

Which then, does it mean it's not white?

My non-black body.

My body that is not English,

yet it could be. Could it?

It could be.

What does my body say to you?

My gay body. My fat body. My sexual body.

My body and its story…

Where does it belong?

This privileged, middle-class body.

This upright, erect, able, thinking body.

Is it presentable?

It is me who stands here in front of you.

Me, whoever that may be.

In a body I don't feel comfortable in.

A body that belongs here, but only

when I force myself to stand here.

He walks to a different spot.

Or here.

He walks upstage left, by the back wall.

Or here. To question.

*

An image of the Beirut skyline from a distance is projected onto the upstage wall.

'Nehna Wel Amar Jiran' by Fairuz plays.

VICTOR turns, straightens the chair, and drags it behind himself upstage, across the image, as if it were a suitcase. As he reaches stage right, he takes the chair centre stage.

He removes the smaller box that is covering the bigger one and helium balloons fly out. He places it on the back of the chair, facing the audience. He uncovers the lens of the mini-projector that faces it. An image is projected onto the piece of cardboard that stands on the visible wooden feet of the chair. Together they become an old television.

VICTOR:

Years ago, long before I moved to the UK, back in São Paulo, Brazil, we used to drive to the beach town of Guarujá often, on weekends. That's where the Sephardic Jews used to go. And my dad used to insert a cassette into the cassette player, in the car on the way from São Paulo to Guarujá. And the song he often played was called 'Allo Beirut'. Or 'Hello Beirut'. I never knew what it said at the time apart from 'hello, hello, hello Beirut'. He, my dad, would often sing it himself when anyone mentioned Beirut. His hometown. The one he left when he was thirteen.

Later I discovered that the song came out in 1966. One year before my dad left for Brazil. It was sung by Sabah, one of the big divas of the Arabic chanson. And it spoke dearly of a place that was then living a golden era: the Paris of the Middle East. In those days people thought it was cool to be compared to Paris.

Less than a decade after that, a civil war broke out between Maronites and Shiites and anyone and everyone in-between. That's when my mother left, in 1975. The song 'Allo Beirut', I found out later, speaks of someone asking the operator to connect them to the radio station, where they seem to have lost their heart, and their babe. And really their babe here is Beirut as the song mentions many of the neighbourhoods in the city in a very romantic way.

After 1975 'Allo Beirut' became a song of memory, of those glory days. Allo *(clears throat)* allo *(tries again)* allo… *(Starts singing with his eyes closed.)*

He sings 'Allo Beirut'.

Sabah was a real star. She starred in over ninety films throughout her life – according to Wikipedia. She used to wear these outrageous dresses and hairpieces. She actually reminds me of my great-aunt Marcelle, whom I met much later. She left her Jewish roots behind, and from Lebanon moved to Italy. To Rome. And converted to Catholicism. For a man, a diplomat. Sabah and Marcelle were completely similar. They weren't completely similar, but the way they liked to dress up and the big personalities were definitely a thing.

(Two and a half years ago) I went to Beirut for the first time and I saw a city that is partly still in ruins. You can feel the tension in the air. The remnants of a divided country, of a civil war that lasted for the best part of fifteen years. A people who love to party hard to forget and pretend. Streets where you never know if someone is watching you. Empty spaces left by bombs and bullets. And a place where some rich *Khaleeji* Arabs from the neighbouring countries go to let their hair down. To fuck prostitutes. To drink some wine, or *arak*.

VICTOR plays a YouTube video on his laptop that is projected onto the cardboard TV. It is the music video for Sabah's 'Allo Beirut': images of Beirut in the sixties, and Sabah on a bed, on the phone, wearing flamboyant clothes and hairpieces.

The image of the São Paulo skyline fades in on the upstage wall.

On his computer, VICTOR opens a Google Maps image of a skyscraper in São Paulo. It is projected onto the cardboard TV.

In São Paulo we used to live on the seventh floor of an eleven-storey building. That's before we moved to the twenty-eighth floor of a thirty-storey building, when I was thirteen. This is the first building I ever lived in. We used to have this huge television.

I was told not to stay up late. So of course, as soon as my parents went to bed, I would sneak into the living room and *peeeew...* I would turn the TV on. And I would watch these late-night TV series, or *miniséries* as we called them. They were like *novelas*, or soap operas, but with even more sexual content. And they helped soothe me so much over those years. To numb me against the discomfort of being there.

He walks to the microphone.

I'm ten years old. Ari, Beto and I agree through our mothers to throw our first ever disco-party. Mom and I create a black-and-white invitation on my – our – DOS computer. In a software that came with the computer, I choose a graphic and I choose a font. I print it on printer paper, with holes on either side. The printer prints line by line… *Cha cha, cha cha, cha cha.*

I – we – tear the detachable sides of the paper, where the holes are. I – we – fold the square paper twice, and I have an invitation. I distribute it in class and to some friends from Netzah, the youth club I'm a part of. I also invite *madrichim*, the older teenagers who look after us. I wear white Lee jeans, and a denim Lee shirt – tucked in by my mom, or myself, I don't remember which.

I enter the salon on the ground floor of the three-skyscraper complex where Ari lives, which is five streets down the road from our much smaller building. People start arriving but they don't fill up the whole salon. I'm exposed.

At some point the song 'Não Quero Dinheiro' by Tim Maia comes on. Lydia, one of the *madrichot*, knows all the lyrics to it. I love it and dance to it with all I've got. Later on they play it again, by which time I start catching some words. The lyrics speak of not wanting money, just wanting to love. That all week long what this guy has waited for was to love. I don't understand the concept, but I love the song. And I also look for love in that salon…

The image on the wall fades to a postcard of Rio de Janeiro.

VICTOR addresses the audience.

Can you guess what my biggest shame in being Brazilian is?

Audience member replies.

Any other guesses?

Audience member replies.

Since moving to the UK, my biggest shame in being Brazilian is that I can't samba! How many people here can samba?

Audience members raise their hands.

So I have decided that throughout the course of my performances of this show, *Where to Belong*, I will learn how to samba.

1. Can one of the people who raised their hands teach me some samba steps?

An audience member joins VICTOR on stage and teaches him some steps. VICTOR asks the STAGE MANAGER to play some music. A high-speed samba is played. VICTOR thanks the person.

2. As no one can samba here let me introduce you to my friend Michele.

VICTOR plays a samba tutorial on YouTube. He dances some samba.

(To STAGE MANAGER.) Can we have some music?

Some more dancing.

Thank you *(name of STAGE MANAGER)*. Thank you.

VICTOR grabs the helium balloons one by one and distributes them to some audience members as he talks to them.

Can I ask you a question? Do you remember what your favourite food was when you were growing up?

Audience member replies.

(To someone else.) And you?

Audience member replies.

Mine was *kibbeh*, or *quibe* as we call it in Brazil. It's a Lebanese savoury meat parcel made up of wheat and mince and spices, like cumin. And it's deep-fried, which is my favourite part. The type I loved the most was the one we'd only have once a year, around Passover time, or *pessah* as we call it. That's the time when the Jews would have left Egypt, freeing themselves from slavery. The story goes that one Friday Moses came and told everybody that it was time to leave, to escape, and they had to do it immediately. They were all baking their *challa* – the sabbath bread – in the oven in their homes.

There was no time to wait for it to rise. So they took the flatbread with them instead and called it *matzah*.

Because of that, for one week in the year you can't eat regular bread, only *matzah*.

And you can't use regular flour. So they make *matzo kibeh*, out of *matzah* flour. Down the road from us, there used to be this guy called Abadi, who would make some delicious *matzah quibes*. My mom used to think that he was unhygienic. But *vovó* Rosa, my grandma, didn't. So we'd have it in her house every year and I used to love it. Sometimes I'd be thinking of it throughout the year.

Of course I also love Brazilian food: *arroz e feijão, coxinha, pastel, estrogonofe, moqueca*. But I still think Lebanese food is the best. Sorry.

At *vovó* Linda's, my mom's mom, my favourites were *hamod* – potato and lemon stew with rice – and *bamieh* – okra with tomato sauce and rice.

As you know, my mom comes from Beirut. She used to live near the centre of town, and close to the sea. Right in the middle of Rue de Phénicie, or Phoenicia Street.

That's where the shootings started.

One side's militia would fire from the Holiday Inn behind her building toward their enemies on the next street in front of her building. This was October 1975.

As soon as the first shots went off, *vovô* Victor, my grandpa, got the whole family to gather in the hallway by the front door of their apartment on the fourth floor, so they would stay there and sleep there. Palestinian men would bring up bread to them, so they could survive. A few days later it was my mom's fifteenth birthday. She ran to her bedroom and prepared a suitcase with some of her favourite things to take when they fled. Among them were photos of herself and family.

VICTOR pops the balloon he's been holding with a pin. He grabs the balloons he gave the audience and pops them one by one.

'These are the fireworks to celebrate your birthday, Dani,' said *vovô* Victor after they heard the bombs.

A few days later, a man *vovô* Victor paid to get them out of the war came to pick them up. Mom went to her bedroom quickly and brought her suitcase to the door. The man asked what that was. She said they were her things to take. He said she couldn't take anything. And so, wearing as many clothes as she could fit on her body, she ran down the stairs with her parents and the man.

When they got out of the building they turned left and reached the corner where they had to run from one building to the next praying not to be shot.

The man told *vovó* Linda to run. So she did. He told *vovô* Victor next. But he said he'd only run after he saw his daughter go first. So she ran. Then him. Then the man. They turned right in the next street where a car was waiting to take them to the airport. And out of the country. Mom never forgot.

She never returned to Beirut.

This is me forty-two years later, in her flat.

VICTOR goes to the computer and plays a clip of himself FaceTiming his mother and showing her the different rooms in the flat. She is in a car in São Paulo with his sister. As she sees her old home, she responds mostly with joy, euphoria and nostalgia.

This clip is played out to its completion throughout the next section.

VICTOR walks to the microphone. He takes a piece of paper from his pocket. He reads from it.

It's an evening in January of 2017. I'm thirty-four.

I have been in Beirut for eleven days. I have visited many memory places where my family used to hang out or be. I've visited the Jewish cemetery in Sodeco, the old, now-refurbished synagogue in Wadi Abu Jamil – an area of the city where not one old building stands as a result of wars, gentrification and corruption. I've also seen an openly anti-Semitic book displayed in the main bookshop in Hamra.

My foot aches as if it's broken, even if it's not. My glands are swollen. My whole body has responded to this place. The historical trauma. The fond and loving memories told to me, that have become a part of me. To see this place. Hear the language. Taste the food. Experience the music. See the street names, and the older ladies walking the streets, reminding me of my grandmother. The local humour reminding me of my dad. The abandoned synagogue on the mountains, in Bhamdoun, where I saw abandoned clothes on the floor, possibly left by recent Syrian refugees.

I've eaten at the Sporting Club restaurant several times, the place where mom used to go to swim. I hear about Israel having destroyed this country more than once. Wars and battles. Also, the contemporary denial of a city of so much pain. Beirut. I've seen.

I came with my boyfriend. He's scared. A member of Amal – a political group that has been called terrorist – stopped him, took a photo of his ID as he was filming Phoenicia Street at my request.

I'm staying with Jihad, my Muslim Lebanese-Sierra Leonean-British friend whom I met ten years previous at the George and Dragon, a gay pub in Shoreditch, London. His boyfriend and mine go back to London at some point.

Jihad has a friend who lives in the building where my mom used to live in. His friend's flatmate invites us for coffee. I call my mom from his flat. Her actual flat is on the fourth floor, but we're on the third. This guy knows the woman who lives in mom's old flat.

She lets us in later that day. I bring my suitcase with me as it's the last day of my trip.

I FaceTime mom. Jihad films us. I show her the dining room and she wants to see the living room that leads onto the terrace. She's in her car, driving, in São Paulo, with my sister next to her.

She gets ecstatic as she recognizes the rooms I show her. And so do I. I'm so excited to connect with her.

I show her the terrace that leads to the outside of her bedroom. I want to show her things she can recognize. She doesn't respond to the room from outside but once I go inside and show her the view outward towards the windows she used to look out of as a child she squeals with joy, louder than she has been. She tells my sister, who's next to her, to look at the hallway as she laughs and laughs and I'm so happy.

I show her the two hotels that she has named all these years as a reference to what was around where she lived, the Martinez and the Phoenicia.

Her living room is now an artist's studio. Her bedroom, where she used to sleep with three siblings, is now a second living room. She wants to see her parents' room, her grandma's room.

When we get to the now-refurbished bathroom, as she tells me the bathtub was somewhere else, the battery in the camera dies.

I show her the rest of the flat briefly and then make my way to the airport. She later thanks me for what she calls the biggest gift I could have ever given her.

*

VICTOR walks toward the TV and kneels next to it.

After leaving Lebanon my mother spent a year in Paris, where her most vivid memory is of the tiny flat she stayed in, where her sister was living. The shared toilet, outside the flat, at the end of the corridor. It being many floors up and there being no lift. And the woman in the market telling her mother, as she touched the tomatoes to decide which one to buy: *'bas les pattes'* or 'put away your paws'.

After that year they all moved to Houston, Texas, apart from her sister. That's where my mother lived for the next five years before marrying dad.

There she studied in a majority-black school where she felt threatened and different. In the flat she lived with her family also lived her uncle Theo, an unmarried man who worked at the gas station where *vovô* Victor also worked.

Her parents, my grandparents, used to say that uncle Theo would give away cigarettes to good-looking men at the station. And maybe he'd give them more than that. Back in Lebanon he supposedly ran film sessions in his flat, or X-rated film sessions. He would have one for the adults, the married couples, and another one for the young men. Or so I'm told. He also used to pay much more attention to my uncles than he ever did to my mom.

That's when it's assumed mom developed her homophobia and racism. Or who knows how these things come about? And with having moved around so much, she also developed a fear of change, of any kind.

VICTOR makes his way to the microphone.

*

A blue screen is projected onto the upstage wall.

It's circa 1997. I'm in a swimming pool on the outskirts of a main city in Israel. There are Peruvians, Chileans, French people, and people from many other countries. We're a group from São Paulo consisting of ten boys. All straight as far as I know.

I stare at guys for a little bit. But really what catches my attention is a group of girls. All fair. Smiling. Their portable stereo playing a cassette. They know all the words to the song. I've never heard it before and I want to know what it is. One girl sits on another's shoulders. They move their arms from one side to the other.

Three years later I move to England. One day, at the Virgin Megastore on the corner of Oxford Street and Tottenham Court Road, I hear that same song and remember those girls.

How I wanted to be their friend. To establish some connection. To hang out. Talk about the boys. Pull the boys. How I wanted to get away from the football players in my group. The girl-seekers. The bad jokers. But I'm ashamed to reach out. This is a place where young Jews from all around the world gather. We're all here to be told about the importance of Israel in our lives. To fall in love with it. To mingle with other Jews. Even if we don't.

Three years later at the Virgin Megastore on the corner of Oxford Street and Tottenham Court Road, I hear that same song. I ask the guy who works there and I buy the album that features it. The *Best Of* of the group that sings it.

VICTOR steps out of the microphone and addresses the audience as he picks up an LED light, plugs it and sets it for the next section.

It was never going to be cool for me to have sung that girls' song. And it still feels a bit wrong. But I can play my CD in my flat in Kilburn Park, which I was told was Maida Vale, and I can learn all the words to it. And I can be as much of a girl as I want to be.

But I'm not being a girl. Just myself. In this new-found freedom. In my living room. No one around. In London. The gayest city in the world.

He turns his back to the audience. 'Never Ever' by All Saints plays. He dances. Small steps get bigger. At the line 'you can tell me to my face' he looks at the audience and carries on.

The line 'I feel isolated' is repeated three times – like a broken record. VICTOR turns to face the audience and looks down. The song stops playing.

He starts to run around the TV as if from someone.

My dad used to come home late from work, and he'd often catch me hitting my brother. Or my mom would tell him.

We used to have this big round glass dinner table in the living room. So as soon as I heard the door I'd run to the furthest side away from him as possible. And he'd chase me. And I'd run. And I was never caught.

He continues running as the audio starts. He then starts to slow down.

As the following pre-recorded audio plays, VICTOR dismounts the set, using all objects to create a barrier between him and the audience. He starts with the TV box, then projector, laptop; he moves boxes and chair and table and light and cassette player and so on.

The following plays in VICTOR's voice:

It's the 19th of April of 2017. I sit in my studio at CASA Theatre Festival's headquarters planning new scenes for this show, *Where to Belong*. I get a bout of inspiration. Lots of ideas are flowing.

It's the 19th of April of 2017 and my daddy is in town, or *papi* as I call him, papi is in town, on the way back from Israel where he spent Passover with our whole immediate family: my mom, my brother and my sister, also my brother's wife and his four children and my sister's husband and her son. They spent it in family, in Jerusalem.

I was half-invited to join them. I was told that they would stop here, on the way back, papi and mami, and that they would of course spend time with me and my partner...

And he asked me if I would go to Israel to meet them, which I wasn't sure if I would have the time for because of work. He asked if I would go and I then realized that he was asking about me, but not my partner, who I lived with, because my sister-in-law didn't know about it, he said. Because he had asked my brother and he had said that she didn't know about it. My brother is religious – 'Well if she doesn't know about it tell her,' I said. 'It's not just like that,' he said.

Previously he had said that they couldn't have me come out so my brother and sister would not risk losing pretenders to marry in the community. He had also said for a long while that my mother was not okay with it and he had to protect her. He has said that of others several times. To protect them. To wait…

We don't have all the time in the world, papi. We HAVE made progress, but what wasted times. What cost it has been to postpone things.

When I was a child, my brother was born with an issue in his elbow, some kind of infection that ate it up. He couldn't stretch his arm or fold it. Daddy blamed it on me at first. I used to hit my brother often, and daddy would arrive home and hit me back. Chase me around the table.

I don't know if where we grow up is where we feel most at home. To belong. Where? To belong? I found my way here. With his money I found my way here. And I built it myself. My own world. My fortress. My bunker.

I don't see papi in this trip. Not him nor mom. I had made it clear even before they went to Israel. I made it crystal clear and found it strange they took it in so quickly and just wished me all the best. Until this morning when I get a message from mom saying: 'We'll be at the Dorchester at two p.m., look forward to seeing you.' No. You won't be seeing me. This is my home. And I'll protect it with all I've got. This is my home. At least for the time being.

VICTOR undoes the red tape that fixes the microphone to the stand. He uses it to finish the barrier by making a line on the floor.

He sets the chair in the middle of the space. He grabs the cassette tape recorder, places it on top of the chair, and brings the microphone to it. He presses play.

*

VICTOR's questions and answers from members of the audience play. These are the recordings made at the start of the show as the audience came in. Ideas of belonging, home, memories from childhood and a song are heard. He listens.

*

As the recording ends, VICTOR places the tape recorder on the floor. He sits on the chair and speaks to the audience.

When I was a child I used to watch Holocaust films. And war films. And I'd always wonder why they didn't leave… Why did they stay until the worst happened? Now – having been to places and spoken to people who stayed throughout wars, and having a bit more maturity to understand financial conditions, connections, courage, outlooks upon life – I would say that some people just hope for the best. Some are okay with living through the troubles. Some have no choice. Some have a death wish. And so many other reasons…

But since we're all here today, I want to suggest we do a bit of planning. So we can make an informed choice.

Please take a moment and think, if you ever had to move out of where you live, of your city, overnight, what's the one place you would go to?

After a moment.

If you'd stay no matter what that's also a choice.

One more moment.

Now can you please take your phones out and either write it down in the Notes app or on a text. If you don't have a phone with you, you could ask for some help from your neighbour.

After a moment.

Now, think of two people you'd take with you, or who you'd make sure got somewhere safe. And write them down.

After a moment.

Now think of three things you would take with you.

After a moment.

VICTOR picks up the microphone and speaks into it.

Portugal. Yorgos and Phoebe. A notebook with poems I wrote when I was a teenager. My hard drive with writings and archive of my work. An album with photos from different times in my life.

(To the audience.) Would anyone else like to share theirs?

He hands the microphone to a member of the audience. They reply.

Someone else?

Audience members reply.

One more?

Audience member replies.

VICTOR walks back centre stage. He places the mic on the floor.

He takes out a folded piece of paper from his back pocket and reads from it.

(Eleven months ago) I was in São Paulo with my partner for the first time, and I took him to some of my favourite places where I used to hang out or be when I was growing up. My first home in Rua São Vicente de Paula. The second flat I lived in, down the road. Ari's three-skyscraper complex in Rua Tupi.

The Italian restaurant Jardim de Napoli. Sushi Kyo in Vila Mariana. My school in Jardins where you can't see anything, since they put up a really tall wall and massive blocks of cement in the pavement, after a synagogue in Buenos Aires was bombed in the '90s.

We also went by the synagogues Beit Yaacov and Mekor Haim, and even the one in Bela Cintra, where I had my bar mitzvah.

I messaged many uncles, aunts and some cousins who I was in touch with, and said I was around with my boyfriend. They all invited us over for coffee or a meal. And it really felt like progress.

After a bit of negotiation, as I have my boundaries with my parents now – I mean we weren't invited for the family Rosh Hashanah dinner with my brother and sister – I agreed to join them and my sister and her family for the last Rosh Hashanah lunch, at my parents' place.

And in the background, there was this shift in the politics and society of the place. The elections were on and you couldn't help but notice it. Homophobic discourse was on the rise. And since then, their far-right candidate has been elected.

My friends were seriously thinking of moving out of the country to somewhere where they'd feel safer.

One day before coming back to London, when Yorgos, my partner, went to buy some local photographs to use in his work, I sat in a *padaria*. Eating *pão na chapa with requeijão*, or bread with Brazilian cream cheese, I remembered growing up in that place, in the '80s and '90s, when Brazil was just coming out of a dictatorship.

(Ten months ago), on the final election day, I was on WhatsApp with my sister and I asked her 'the question'. She replied that she strongly believed that our parents had voted for the new government.

VICTOR addresses the audience.

You know. My parents really looked after me financially. Yet I realised something. That I've always had this deep craving. This wish. That's summed up in that song they played in my first ever disco-party. When I was ten. At Ari's party salon. The one we threw with Beto.

And it went:

VICTOR sings 'Não Quero Dinheiro' by Tim Maia as a gentle lament.

'I was waiting all week long. To see you smiling. To see you singing. When we love we don't think about money. We just want to love.

No way at all. I don't want money. I want sincere love. That's what I hope for. And I shout out to the world. I don't want money. I just want to love.'

He goes upstage right, taking the chair with him. He places it straight in front of him, and drags it across the image of Beirut projected onto the wall like a suitcase. (The opposite journey he did in the beginning of the show.) Fairuz plays.

*

VICTOR places the cassette player on top of the chair as it was set in the beginning of the show and addresses the audience.

So to finish us off I'll get on with the closing, or the epilogue, or whatever you wanna call it.

Epilogue

VICTOR:

Am I allowed to place my body in this space?

Would you embrace my white body?

Would you embrace my Jewish body,

that is not English?

Would you embrace my gay body?

Would you embrace my fat body?

Would you embrace my sexual body?

Would you embrace my privileged, middle-class body?

Would you embrace my upright, erect, able,

thinking body?

This body I don't feel comfortable in.

If it's me standing here in front of you.

Will you embrace me?

He pleads to one audience member.

Will you hold me?

And you, will you hold me?

And you, and you, and you. Will you hold me?

Audience members walk up to the stage and embrace VICTOR. 'Não Quero Dinheiro' comes on.

The end.

WWW.OBERONBOOKS.COM

First published in 2019 by Oberon Books Ltd
521 Caledonian Road, London N7 9RH
Tel: +44 (0.) 20 7607 3637 / Fax: +44 (0.) 20 7607 3629
e-mail: info@oberonbooks.com
www.oberonbooks.com

PB ISBN: 9781786827647
E ISBN: 9781786827630

Cover Photo: *Wondrous Vulva* by Michael Wharley and Rebecca Pitt /
My World Has Exploded A Little Bit by Rebecca Pitt and Matthew
Richardson

eBook conversion by Lapiz Digital Services, India.

Bella Heesom

REJOICING AT HER WONDROUS VULVA THE YOUNG WOMAN APPLAUDED HERSELF

T0347916

OBERON BOOKS
LONDON

WWW.OBERONBOOKS.COM

An **All About You** production, commissioned by Ovalhouse, and supported by Arts Council England and the Peggy Ramsay Foundation.

Premiered at the downstairs theatre, Ovalhouse, London, 13th May 2019 (previews from 9th May) with the following company:

Bella Heesom – Writer & Performer: Ego/Brain/Writer

Bella trained as an actor at LAMDA, after studying philosophy at the University of Cambridge. She founded All About You with Donnacadh O'Briain. Her debut play as a writer, *My World Has Exploded A Little Bit*, toured nationally following critical acclaim at the Edinburgh Fringe and VAULT Festivals. She was invited by Newnham College, Cambridge, to give a Tedx talk: *Why it's Rational to be Emotional*. She also hosts a podcast: *Rejoicing With Bella*. Bella has enjoyed lead roles and ensemble work in theatre, film and TV projects, including Pandora in *The Woman in The Moon* (Sam Wanamaker Playhouse); numerous parts in *PEEP* (Edinburgh and Latitude festivals) and Zainab in *Mathematics of the Heart* (Best New Play, Brighton Fringe & Theatre 503).

For more, see bellaheesom.com.

Sara Alexander – Performer: Appetite/Clitoris/Actor

It's been so wonderful to work on this show from its embryonic stage, contributing to its growth over a couple of years; from its five minute incarnations which we trawled around experimental theatre nights, to its current, joyous, unfurling.

Other favourite things: cooking at the allotment, crunchy conversation and fierce coffee that grows hairs on my chest (chin?). Factoids: University of Bristol & DSL graduate. Work includes: projects for the RSC, National and Globe Theatre Rome, *Harry Potter & the Deathly Hallows 1,* Zeffirelli's *Sparrow, Mysti Show* & *Hounded (series regular BBC)*. Harper Collins publishes my novels *Under a Sardinian Sky, The Secret Legacy* and *The Last Concerto*, stories with a distinctly Italian flavour and ardent female protagonists.

For all other musings: www.saraalexander.net @SaraJAlexander

Donnacadh O'Briain – Director & Dramaturg
Donnacadh's productions have played at The Royal
Shakespeare Company, in the West End, and internationally.
His acclaimed production of *Rotterdam* by Jon Brittain won
the 2017 Olivier Award for Outstanding Achievement in an
Affiliate Theatre. He developed and directed All About You's
first production; *My World Has Exploded A Little Bit.*

Other favourite productions include: *Always Orange* by Fraser
Grace (RSC); *Electrolyte* (Edinburgh Festival & touring) *Mother
Christmas* (Hampstead); *PEEP* (Edinburgh and Latitude
festivals); *King Lear* (Wexford Opera House and touring); and
as an Assistant director to the RSC's multi award-winning
Histories Cycle.

Liz Ranken – Movement Director
Awards: Place Portfolio Award; Capital Award; Time Out
Award for bringing theatre alive with movement. Liz was
Artist in Residence at the CCA in Glasgow and was a founder
member of DV8 Physical Theatre. Choreography/movement
director credits include: *The History Cycle* (d. Michael Boyd);
Complete Works cycle & many others at the RSC, where
she's an Associate Artist, *Orfeo* (Royal Opera House at The
Roundhouse); *Eugene Onegin* and *Palléas* (Garsington Opera);
Teddy Ferrera (Donmar Warehouse); *Cunning Little Vixen* (The
Byre Theatre); *The Crucible* and *Orlando* (The Royal Exchange,
Manchester); *The Cherry Orchard* (Bristol Old Vic); *Don
Giovanni* (Garsington Opera); Beltane Festival Edinburgh, and
site specific performances with NVA in Scotland and the band
Test Department.

Film & TV choreography & performance include: *Alive and
Kicking, Touched, Dance for Camera* (BBC2, Gold Cup Award
winner); *Edward II* (d. Derek Jarman); *Caught Looking*
(d. Constantine Giannaris, shown at MOMA). Humanitarian
projects include: choreography & performance with CAT
A, working with prisoners, The Big Tease, working with
Strippers and Ooh working with performers with and without
a disability.

Liz paints professionally and she has had a portrait in The Heinz archive at The National Portrait Gallery, and a painting in The Portrait Collection at the RSC.

www.elizabethranken.com Instagram: lizrankenart

Elizabeth Harper – Set and Costume Design

Elizabeth is delighted to reunite with Bella, Donnacadh and Sara. Making theatre is a wonderful opportunity to address topics we are often unable to confront in "real life," and share with each other in a safe space. *Wondrous Vulva* does just this: it bravely and openly explores female sexuality, it confronts the male gaze, but all the while questioning, learning and rejoicing in the journey. It is a piece of work that puts so much positivity into the world and it has been such a privilege to help create.

Elizabeth has been designing theatre around the UK for five years, as well as undertaking many fine art commissions for both private and corporate clients.

Jess Bernberg – Lighting Design

Designs include: *Out of Water, Cougar* (Orange Tree Theatre); *The Crucible, Sex Sex Men Men, A New and Better You, Buggy Baby* (The Yard); *The Town That Trees Built* (Young Vic); *And the Rest of Me Floats* (Birmingham Rep/Bush Theatre); *The Borrowers* (Tobacco Factory); *Fabric, Drip Feed* (Soho Theatre); *Victoria's Knickers, Consensual* (NYT); *Medusa, Much Ado About Nothing, Dungeness, Love and Information* (Nuffield Southampton Theatres); *Homos* (Finborough Theatre); *SongLines* (HighTide); *Devil with the Blue Dress, FCUK'D* (OffWestEnd Award nomination) (The Bunker).

Awards: 2017 Association of Lighting Designer's Francis Reid Award.

Candice Weaver – Sound Design
Candice is a graduate of RADA's Sound Design for Theatre postgraduate course, and has previously completed a degree in Music. Previous sound designs include the Southwark Playhouse, Arcola Theatre, the Edinburgh Fringe, and various UK tours. When not sound designing, Candice's engineering work also includes the National Theatre, the Royal Opera House, and can mostly be found in West End theatres looking after microphones and mixing shows.

Hannah Elsy – Producer
Producing includes: *The Quentin Dentin Show* (Arts Theatre, Tristan Bates, Rich Mix, National Theatre Studio); The Quentin Dentin Show Original Cast Recording, available on iTunes, Spotify etc; *Queen Cunt Sacred or Profane* (UK Tour); *Summer Nights In Space* (VAULT Festival); *I Have A Bad Feeling About This* (VAULT Festival). Hannah general managed *Ishq The Musical* (Sadler's Wells); and booked the recent UK tours of *The Shy Manifesto* and Extant's *Flight Paths*. Hannah works in the Old Vic's finance team as Administrative Projects Coordinator. Coming up: *Everything Is Absolutely Fine* (Manchester Lowry & UK Tour).

Timothy Kelly – Production Manager and Video Associate
Timothy Kelly is a technical theatre creative, working across lighting, video and production management. He is particularly passionate about accessibility in theatre and has built a creative captioning engine for shows with d/Deaf and hearing casts, and built an app to help enable people with severe learning disabilities to operate lighting and sound.

Recent credits include: *Electrolyte* (Lighting, UK Tour); *Sirens* (Lighting & Projection, UK Tour); *The Noises* (Lighting, Old Red Lion); *Orangutan* (Lighting & Production Manager, VAULT); *Jade City* (Lighting & Set, VAULT); *17* (Projection & Lighting, VAULT); *The Trench* (Associate Lighting, Southwark Playhouse).

Maria Gurevich – Technical Stage Manager

Having got a degree in World Literature and Linguistics from the Moscow State University, Maria moved to the UK and graduated from the Guildhall School of Music; Drama with a BA Honours in Technical Theatre.

Credits include: DSM on *Un Ballo in Maschera* and *Il Segreto di Susanna* (Opera Holland Park); *The Barber of Seville* (Grange Festival) and *Devil With The Blue Dress* (Bunker Theatre); CSM on *Book on Aladdin* (QDos, Beck Theatre); technical SM on *Hear Me Raw* (Soho Theatre and Arcola Theatre) and the award-nominated *Kieran Hodgson: Maestro* (Soho Theatre). Maria has also produced dozens of shows at the Edinburgh Fringe with the Berk's Nest production company.

Martha J. Baldwin – Assistant Director

Martha has previously assisted on productions at her hometown theatre, Ilkley Playhouse (West Yorkshire) and has directed her own work alongside of her course at Central Saint Martins. She is currently writing and preparing her graduation show, opening in May 2020. She has a great interest in female led work and movement direction.

THANKS

Donnacadh, for sharing my excitement and ambition for an important but nebulous idea and helping me birth it. For knowing when to speak, and when to stop and listen, and for wanting to learn. Sara – I couldn't have dreamt up a more open, generous, engaged, loving, funny, grounded playmate. You inspire me. The show wouldn't be what it is without you. Liz Ranken, for helping me to unleash my instinctive, feral self, and connect with my body. Max Sobol – you're a star, and Raquel Meseguer for helping us to begin. The entire creative team – thank you for helping me make this a reality, for making it such a joyous process, and for welcoming my baby into the rehearsal room!

Owen Calvert-Lyons and the team at Ovalhouse, David Lockwood and the team at The Bike Shed theatre, Emma Blackman and Roland Smith at Theatre Deli, Shaelee Rooke, Sharp Teeth at Theatre 503, Matt Maltby, Pint Sized at The Bunker, Brian Logan at Camden People's Theatre. The Peggy Ramsay Foundation, and Arts Council England, for making this type of work possible.

All of the women who filled in questionnaires or spoke to me in person about their personal experiences. Emily Nagoski, Naomi Wolf, Nancy Friday, Germaine Greer, Wendy Jones, Rash Dash, Alice Birch, Ella Hickson. Everyone who came to the First Bite shows, filled in feedback forms, and shared so generously in the discussions afterwards.

ALL ABOUT YOU is the creative collaboration between writer/performer Bella Heesom and Olivier Award-winning director/dramaturg Donnacadh O'Briain. Our work is characterised by a playful approach to big themes. We strive to cultivate empathy by exposing our common humanity, in all its raw, flawed fragility and beauty. We create theatre with the audience experience as the central focus, using a flexible fourth wall, and audience interaction. Our plays combine unflinching emotional honesty, intellectual rigour, and a good dose of silliness, to invite audiences to delve deep inside themselves, find the soft, shadowy parts, and explore them with curiosity and kindness.

ALL ABOUT YOU was formed in 2015 following our years of fruitful collaboration as actor and director on a number of diverse projects. The first play we made together was Bella's debut as a writer: *My World Has Exploded A Little Bit*, a tragi-comic account of Bella's battle with grief following the deaths of her parents. The show received audience, critical and industry acclaim at the Edinburgh Festival Fringe 2016, followed by a Highly Commended run at VAULT Festival, and a successful national tour in 2017, supported by Arts Council England.

'A genuinely valuable piece of work'
Scotsman

'radical honesty and honest artistry'
★★★★★ *Edinburgh Spotlight*

See **bellaheesom.com** for reviews, production photos, trailers, short films etc.

Ovalhouse is a lively theatre in Oval, south London. For the past 50 years, Ovalhouse has been a home to experimental, radical and overlooked artists seeking to make theatre and performance that speaks to a world beyond the mainstream. A hotbed of artistic activism, Ovalhouse is a vital home for boundary-pushing art and artists with an eye on the future. With a theatre programme in two spaces they commission, co-produce and programme innovative work by early career and established artists. Ovalhouse invests in exploration and development, providing a space where artists can develop their creative practice and audiences can encounter new work. **Ovalhouse.com @ovalhouse**

Director	Deborah Bestwick
Executive Producer	Stella Kanu
General Manager	Gary Johnson
Head of Theatre and Artist Development	Owen Calvert-Lyons
Head of Communications and Audience Development	Monique Baptiste-Brown
Operations Manager	Alex Clarke
Technical Manager	Ina Berggren
Finance Manager	Yaw Manu
Manager	
Demonstrate Project Manager	Elena Molinaro
Finance Assistant	Kwame T B Antwi
Press and Digital Marketing Officer	Sophie London
House Managers	Lily Batikyan
	Steph Prior
	James York

Bella Heesom & Sara Alexander as Brain & Clitoris
Photographer Lidia Crisafulli

Characters

EGO / BRAIN / WRITER

APPETITE / CLITORIS / ACTOR

Notes on the text

Words aligned right, in **BOLD CAPS** are to be projected, ideally accompanied by a sound effect as they appear.

Lines in "*italics inside speech marks*" are pre-recorded speech played over the sound system.

/ indicates interruption by another character

– indicates an unfinished thought

The characters of Brain and Clitoris wear big silly hats in the shape of a brain and a clitoris (including all of the internal parts). Ideally, these will be flown in and out of the rig as required, so that putting the hats on and taking them off is quick and seamless.

Most of the action of the play is metaphorical, in that it represents internal conflict between different parts of a person. Therefore, the primary aim of the set design should not be to naturalistically depict the locations of the scenes in the external world. The playing area should be an abstract space, capable of intimacy and expansiveness. The primary ambition of the designer should be to create a warm, welcoming environment that exists outside the male gaze. (Depending on the societal context, this will probably be impossible, but it is still worth striving for.)

The actors' breaths should form part of the storytelling during the dances and the moments when Appetite is referred to as a lion cub/lioness. The use of miniature mics may be appropriate.

For the women who need this.
You are not broken. You are brilliant.

SCENE 1: Bedroom shared with partner. EGO and APPETITE are late 20s here. APPETITE is physically weak and at a distance from EGO. Throughout the scene, she is trying to bridge the gap, and make contact with EGO. EGO does not acknowledge her presence until the very end. EGO is addressing her partner, out front.

EGO:

APPETITE:

I'm sitting on the bed with you, and my mouth's sealed shut. By not taking in any air, I'm shrinking myself. But I'm not invisible. You're looking at me. You're looking at me like I'm a stranger. The fierce woman you admire and lust after has shrunk into a small, strange, silent thing you don't recognise.

struggling to breathe quietly gasping for air

the gasps turn into quiet sobs

silently crying

You're waiting for me to speak. You've raised the topic in a gentle, respectful, way. You want to know what I think about this.

silently shaking

searching, exposed

silent, still, shrunken and exhausted

Why don't I have any thoughts? Where have my thoughts gone? The silence is roaring in my ears, like that really loud silence at the start of an exam when I think it'll deafen me, until I read a question and all my thoughts come flooding in, cascading and dancing and forming themselves into lines of argument.

Except the silence and the blankness   *weakly straining*
are just going on and on. The only
thought I have is really just, please
stop. Please let me out of this
conversation. It feels like a cage.
I've got nothing to say. I'll only
disappoint you. I really don't want   *quietly retching*
to disappoint you. I feel sick. Sick
with worry about what you think of
me. This is an unfamiliar sensation
and I don't know what to do with
it. I want to not care. That's what I
would usually do – not care what
you think of me, because I know
I'm right. But somehow, I feel all
wrong.

retching
guttural groan   *retching*

                                          makes physical contact
                                          with EGO

I wasn't always like this. I used to be
fun. I used to be– when I was little,
it was lush, I used to–
turns towards APPETITE

DANCE 1 – APPETITE & EGO: TWINS IN THE WOMB, TENDER, SHARED, BEAUTIFUL. BOTH HAVE THEIR EYES CLOSED THROUGHOUT. STANDING SIDE BY SIDE, TOUCHING, EGO STRETCHING UP. APPETITE NUZZLING INTO HER SIDE, MOVING IN FRONT OF HER, REACHING BACK AND UP FOR EGO'S HAND, BRINGING IT TO HER FACE. STRETCHING OUT AGAIN, BRINGING EGO'S HAND TO HER BELLY. EGO HUGGING HER FROM BEHIND. APPETITE TAKING EGO'S WEIGHT, BENDING FORWARD, SWINGING FROM SIDE TO SIDE, STEPPING FORWARD, CROUCHING DOWN, WHILE MANTAINING FULL BODY CONTACT. THEY SIT ON THE FLOOR, BOTH OF APPETITE'S LEGS OVER ONE OF EGO'S, ARMS AROUND EACH OTHER, HEADS BURIED IN NECKS, CIRCLING FROM THE WAIST. THEY LEAN BACK, FIND EACH OTHER'S FEET, APPETITE'S LEG SWINGS OVER SO THAT THEY ARE FACING EACH OTHER, LEGS WIDE, GROINS CLOSE, FOREHEADS TOUCHING. THEY CIRCLE. SUDDENLY, BOTH EYES OPEN WITH AN INTAKE OF BREATH – THEY SEE EACH OTHER AND BECOME AWARE OF THEIR SEPARATENESS FOR THE FIRST TIME. APPETITE SNIFFS EGO. EGO BRINGS HER HAND TO APPETITE'S FACE. APPETITE NUZZLES INTO IT.

APPETITE as a lion cub, playing with young EGO. APPETITE is almost like a puppy – affectionately nuzzling, licking and bouncing around excitably, and EGO is delighted with her, physically relaxed, happy to indulge her and return her affection. Their breaths are quick and fluttery.

SCENE 2: *Childhood bedroom. EGO & APPETITE are about nine years old. EGO straddles a pillow, rubbing herself against it. (There probably won't be a real pillow on stage, but this is the action.) At the point of climax she goes very still and tense. APPETITE is experiencing the pleasure with EGO, but her actions don't have to be naturalistic, and could be wildly different. However this is expressed, we see them both experience the feelings associated with the words spoken by the other character – everything is shared.*

EGO:	APPETITE:
	Let's play the game
with the pillow?	
	yes
where we pretend	
	yes
we're having	
	sex! yes!
Quick	
	quickly
quickly	
	feathery
tickly	
	warm
flickering	
	flame
rubbing thighs	
	rubbing
skin	
	whispering
tingling	
	rippling roaring
racing, chasing, running	
	thrilling, glowing, flowing, flying
squeezing, holding	
	pulsing
	juddering
gulping	
	tight
pulling taut	
tighter, still, still, still.	
heavy, shaking breaths, slowly slowing down	*heavy, shaking breaths, slowly slowing down*
	quietly content:
	melting
	sinking
	sliding

GIRLS DON'T MASTURBATE

EGO: APPETITE:

Opens her eyes and reads the
words on the wall. Becomes
uncomfortable. Whispers:
What did we do?

                        I don't know.

Our armpits are sticky, why
are our armpits sticky?

                        I don't know.

Our knickers are damp.
Why are our knickers damp?

                        I don't know.

physical discomfort, panicked breaths

goes over to APPETITE

Did we do something bad?

                        We did something… golden.
                        Something shimmering,
                        glimmering… like the sun
                        was inside us for a second.

reunited in physical contact with
APPETITE, she relaxes her body
and breath

GIRLS DON'T MASTURBATE
ONLY BOYS MASTURBATE

SCENE 3. *There will probably be some sort of silly fanfare to introduce BRAIN and CLITORIS and the dramatic tonal shift they represent. Hats on. BRAIN & CLITORIS are about ten years old. BRAIN is reading a teen magazine.*

CLITORIS: Hiii

BRAIN:

CLITORIS: How you doin?

BRAIN:

CLITORIS: You haven't played with me in ages

BRAIN: Sh.

CLITORIS: Do you remember last time?

BRAIN: Sshhh!

CLITORIS: Why? It was lovely...

BRAIN: Just be quiet please.

CLITORIS: But it felt so good!

BRAIN: Ugh. Stop it.

CLITORIS: But you loved it!

BRAIN: Just shut up. Someone might hear you.

CLITORIS: So?

BRAIN: So I don't want them to.

CLITORIS: Why not?

BRAIN: Because it's gross!

CLITORIS: What is?

BRAIN: You know...

CLITORIS: What?

BRAIN: *That.*

CLITORIS: What, playing with me?

BRAIN: Yes!

CLITORIS: Oh.

BRAIN: None of the other girls do it.

CLITORIS: Why not?

BRAIN: They think it's disgusting. Or weird, or something. And like, slutty. Probably. I don't know, but nobody does it.

Beat.

CLITORIS: Boys do, don't they?

BRAIN: Well yeah, but boys are gross.

CLITORIS: Oh.

Beat.

BRAIN: They say you smell like fish.

CLITORIS: Who?

BRAIN: The boys.

CLITORIS: But they've never met me.

BRAIN: Not you specifically, just that… part, of a girl.

CLITORIS: Oh.

Is that bad?

BRAIN: Yes!

CLITORIS: Oh.

Don't they eat fish?

BRAIN: Um, I guess most of them do, yeah.

CLITORIS: Oh.

(WRITER looks to audience. Removes BRAIN hat.)

WRITER: *(To audience.)* Don't laugh at that. Come on, that's beneath you. *(To CLITORIS, gesturing towards CLITORIS hat.)* I think this requires some explanation.

CLITORIS/ACTOR: What, me?

WRITER: Yes.

CLITORIS/ACTOR: Why?

WRITER: Some people might not recognise you.

CLITORIS/ACTOR: Really?

WRITER: Yes. I had no idea you looked like that – for years I only knew about your little head; I only found out about the rest of your body when I was researching this play.

CLITORIS/ACTOR: You thought I was just a head?

WRITER: Yeah.

CLITORIS/ACTOR: Without a body?

WRITER: Yes! Don't look at me like that – how was I supposed to know? No one talks about you.

CLITORIS/ACTOR: *(Hurt.)* No one talks about me?

WRITER: No. Not even in sex ed.

CLITORIS/ACTOR: Why not?

WRITER: Well, some people think you're not that important, because you don't serve a function / in reproduction.

CLITORIS/ACTOR: Excuse me! Don't serve a function! How about intense pleasure, soaring joy, no – ECSTACY! Does transcending the mortal and touching the fucking divine not qualify as a function?! *(To audience.)* Can I get a 'hell yeah'?!

WRITER: Well, exactly. That's why I want to make sure everyone knows all about you.

CLITORIS/ACTOR: Go on then; tell them.

WRITER: Okay. *(To audience.)* Good evening, everyone. Please allow me to introduce my Clitoris.

CLITORIS/ACTOR: Tada!

WRITER: Okay. A quick anatomy lesson: if a female human stands naked in front of the mirror, she sees her mons pubis – the fleshy mound covered in pubic hair. In relation to the clitoris, that's up here.

CLITORIS/ACTOR: I'll play the whole vulva. *(Transforming sounds/gestures.)*

WRITER: Ready? Okay. Below that are the labia majora; the fleshy, hairy outer lips, and inside those are the labia minora; the thinner lips. At the top of the labia minora, the skin makes a little hood over the external part of the clitoris, which is called the glans. It has over eight thousand nerve endings.

CLITORIS/ACTOR: Like a MILLION TINY SPARKLERS all in my little head! Tss! Tss! Tss-tss!

WRITER: Well, eight thousand, but yes. That's the little button that most people are familiar with.

(Indicating CLITORIS/ACTOR's nose:) Below that is the urethral opening, or pee hole. And below that is the vaginal opening.

(CLITORIS/ACTOR opens mouth to indicate position of vaginal opening.)

> The vagina is a muscular tube leading to the womb. It is internal. The collective name for all of the external parts is the vulva. The majority of the clitoris, the bulbs and the crura, are all internal. As you can see, the bulbs extend down and around the vagina.

CLITORIS/ACTOR: Ooh ooh, tell them about when I get excited!

WRITER: When the female is aroused, the clitoris becomes engorged, and the whole vulva expands. The glans becomes erect, and can be stimulated directly from the outside. The bulbs can be stimulated from the inside, through contact with the walls of the vagina.

CLITORIS/ACTOR: So the G-spot is just me again! It's all me!

(Gestures to techie. Music starts, loud. 'I'm Every Woman' by Whitney Houston. CLITORIS breaks into song and dance)

> *(Sung.)* It's all in meeee. Anything you want done baby, I'll do it naturally!

CLITORIS/ACTOR and WRITER dance to the song for a moment. CLITORIS/ACTOR removes the CLITORIS hat. The music fades out, and the action becomes suggestive of two girls dancing playfully in a playground.

SCENE 4. *Playground. EGO and APPETITE are about eleven years old. EGO is on a swing, speaking to a friend. APPETITE is interacting with her in a non-naturalistic way – perhaps lying on the ground and pushing/pulling her feet to make her swing.*

EGO:	APPETITE:
Oooh my God I fancy Jack so much.	Oooh Jack Jack Jack
He just got this haircut where it's floppy on top, but at the back it's shaved really short, and it	Mmmmmm
feels like velvet.	velvety vvvvelllvet
I can spend hours imagining standing with my face really close to his, and	hhhhhhaaaaaahh
reaching around and touching the warm skin	touching touching warm waaarmmm ssskiiiiinnnnnn
in that hollow	hhhholloooooow
in the back of his neck, and then running my fingers up	fffffiiiiingers
through his soft velvety hair, and	ssssoft velvety velllvet
kissing his perfect lips.	kiss kiiiisss
I've never kissed anyone, but	kiisssssss
I think it would be nice.	kissing lips
I'm quite an early developer.	lipssss
Like most girls in my class are still completely flat chested, but I've already got quite	1 l l l lips p p p pssss
big boobs. Or 'secondary sexual characteristics'. That's what they called them in the video we watched at school. We were all excited cos we thought it was going to be about	*stays in the pleasure of imagining kissing Jack*
sex,	sssssexxx sex ssexxx
but it was just about puberty.	

BOYS GET HARD-ONS
GIRLS GET PERIODS

Gets off the swing, moves away from APPETITE and reads the projections

takes pleasure in the feeling of her own body

Apparently, girls grow breasts
in order to attract a mate,
and feed a baby when they
have one. For the boys, it
was all about their willies.
Apparently, they might start
getting involuntary erections,

erectionsss

where they just look at a girl
and up pops a boner. Can you
imagine? Ping! And they have
wet dreams, which is when they
dream they're having sex
and then they actually cum,
so when they wake up their
sheets are all wet! Gross.
Mind you, not as gross as

boOonerr
Ping! Ping ping ping
Wet dreams
dream   sex
dreammmmmm

not listening, in a sexy daydream
very free physicality, sensual
and pleasurable but youthful,
playful and entirely free of self-
consciousness, making physical
contact with EGO

waking up with blood all over
your sheets, which is what
happened to me last week. I
was desperate to be the first
to start my period, but now
I wish it'd piss off. It's really
painful. I'd definitely rather
have a wet dream.

*DANCE 2: APPETITE'S MOVEMENTS ACTIVATE
EGO, THEN BECOME DANCING, INSTINCTIVE,
SENSUAL, PLEASURABLE, ENTIRELY FREE OF SELF-
CONSCIOUSNESS. EGO REFLECTS APPETITE'S
MOVEMENTS, SO THAT THEY ARE DANCING TOGETHER.
IT IS SPONTANEOUS, PERHAPS A BIT SILLY,
NOT TRADITIONALLY SEXY, BUT ENJOYING THE BODY.
SOMETHING OF THE LION CUB EMERGES
AS THEY SNIFF AND NUDGE EACH OTHER WITH
THEIR HEADS, UNTIL THEY COME TOGETHER,
AND MOVE TOGETHER, ENTWINED.*

EGO turns to face the back wall. Watches as these words appear:

SEX = PENIS IN VAGINA
VIRGINITY = PRECIOUS

SCENE 5. *BRAIN & CLITORIS are about twelve. Hats on. BRAIN is
reading a women's magazine.*

CLITORIS: *(Desperate to know.)* What is sex?

BRAIN: It's when a man puts his penis in woman's vagina.

CLITORIS: *(Deeply disappointed.)* Oh.

Beat.

Does it feel nice?

BRAIN: Yes.

CLITORIS: Are you sure?

BRAIN: Yes, everyone knows it's the best thing ever.

CLITORIS: *(Doubtful.)* Really?

BRAIN: Yes. Don't you believe me?

CLITORIS: Well when you put a tampon in it doesn't feel nice.

BRAIN: Oh. Well, I think he sort of moves it around.

Beat.

CLITORIS: Is that it?

BRAIN: What?

CLITORIS: Is that all sex is?

BRAIN: Uum, well I think you kiss and stuff too.

CLITORIS: Ooh, good. Where?

BRAIN: On the lips.

CLITORIS: Which lips?

BRAIN: The ones on your face.

CLITORIS: What about the others?

BRAIN: That's oral sex.

CLITORIS: What's oral sex?

BRAIN: It's when they use their mouth to do stuff, down there.

CLITORIS: What, like singing?

BRAIN: No, like... using their tongue.

CLITORIS: Oooooh. That sounds good. I think oral sex might be my favourite sex.

BRAIN: But that's not real sex, that's just foreplay.

CLITORIS: Does it feel good?

BRAIN: Yes.

CLITORIS: Then why isn't it real sex?

BRAIN: Uum... I guess, because it can't get you pregnant.

CLITORIS: Oh. Do we want to get pregnant?

BRAIN: No. Definitely not. Not until we're much older.

CLITORIS: So why isn't it sex?

BRAIN: I don't know, it's just not official sex. You can do oral without losing your virginity.

CLITORIS: What's virginity?

BRAIN: It's what you have if you haven't had sex with a boy.

CLITORIS: A boy?

BRAIN: Yes.

CLITORIS: What about a girl?

Beat.

BRAIN: I guess that's not Officially Sex, because you haven't had a willy in your fanny.

CLITORIS: So you only lose your virginity if you have Official Sex?

BRAIN: Yes. And it's very precious, so you don't want to give it away too easily, because you can never get it back.

CLITORIS: Never?

BRAIN: No.

CLITORIS: Who takes it?

BRAIN: The boy you have sex with.

CLITORIS: Why won't he give it back? Is he a thief?

BRAIN: No, he can't. That's not how it works.

CLITORIS: And it's really precious?

BRAIN: Yes.

CLITORIS: Is it shiny?

BRAIN: No.

CLITORIS: Does it sparkle?

BRAIN: No, it's not a *thing.*

CLITORIS: It's not a thing?

BRAIN: No!

CLITORIS: Then how can you lose it?

BRAIN: Well you don't really. It's just– saying you've lost your
virginity is like saying that you're different after you've
had sex.

CLITORIS: Different in a bad way?

BRAIN: Well, you lose your innocence.

CLITORIS: What's innocence?

BRAIN: It's sort of like naivety.

CLITORIS: What's naivety?

BRAIN: It's when you're inexperienced and you don't really
know how the world works.

CLITORIS: What's so precious about that?

Beat.

BRAIN: I think it makes you sort of *pure.* And men find it
attractive.

EGO turns towards the back wall. Watches as these words appear:

YOU ARE A SEX OBJECT

SCENE 6. *A playground. EGO and APPETITE are about thirteen years old. EGO is on a swing, talking to a friend. APPETITE is connected to her, but less intimately than in Scene 4. Perhaps she stands behind, pushing her.*

EGO:

So yesterday, I'm walking to school, yeah? The sun's shining, I've done all my homework, I'm feeling pretty confident that I'll ace my maths test. I'm feeling good, right?

Suddenly,
(Horn honking sound.)
a horn honks right in my ear, like it was so loud, I swear I almost fell over. So, I look, and there's this white van going really fast, and I just hear this guy yell out the window:

"Oi oi! Legs eleven!"

So random. I'm like, having a heart attack 'cause of how loud his horn was, and he's just, like, shouting about my legs.

Beat.

I have got quite nice legs, to be fair. My grandma says I've got aristocratic ankles, 'cause they're so slim.

APPETITE:

*humming happily
enjoying the feeling of the sun
on her face*

she is startled, but finds it funny

relaxed laughter

*she admires/enjoys her legs
– maybe stroking them and/
or playfully kicking them or
jumping about*

21

Anyway, I've just recovered
from the shock, when I almost
walk into someone. This
massive guy's just stopped
dead in the middle of the
pavement. So, I look up, and
he's literally drooling. Like he
doesn't look at me at all, he
just stares down at my boobs
as if they're a pair of Krispy
Kremes, and goes:

"Oh, hello – look at those beauties!"

So weird. So, I just laugh   *looks down at her breasts*
and walk around him, like,   *appreciatively, maybe touches*
whatever. But to be fair, I   *them*
caught sight of myself in
a shop window just after,
and I was walking pretty
quickly – you know I always
walk quickly, and my boobs
were bouncing up and down   *smiling, mesmerised by at the*
quite a lot. Like, it was a bit   *sight of her breasts bouncing in*
Baywatch.   *the shop window impressed:*
                                     Wow
Beat.

Maybe I should walk slower.
I'm always running late,
though.

Gets off the swing and moves away
from APPETITE

Anyway, that wasn't even
the end of it. As I go round
the corner, I see a load of
scaffolding, and all these
builders stop what they're doing
and just stare at me and start
whistling and cheering and stuff.   *laughs*
(Wolf whistles and cat calls.)
I mean, thanks and
everything, but I didn't really   *basks in the positive attention*
do anything that deserves   *shimmies with pleasure*
cheering, I'm just walking to   *enjoys how amazing her body is*
school. I don't know what's so
amazing about that.

***DANCE 3 – EGO BECOMES INCREASINGLY
UNCOMFORTABLE WITH THE EYES OF THE
BUILDERS ON HER. SQUIRMING, TRYING TO HIDE.
SIMULTANEOUSLY, APPETITE IS ENJOYING THE
ATTENTION, AND THE WAY HER BODY MOVES,
PROUDLY DANCING IN THE SPOTLIGHT, BEING
PLAYFUL AND HAVING FUN. HER MOVEMENTS
ARE SPONTANEOUS AND SURPRISING. EGO SEES
HER CONFIDENCE, AND, JEALOUS, TRIES TO
COMPETE BY DOING GENERIC 'SEXY' DANCING. IT'S
UNCOMFORTABLY FORCED. APPETITE STOPS DANCING;
EGO HAS TAKEN THE FUN OUT OF IT. APPETITE
RETREATS. LEFT ON HER OWN, AND FEELING
EXPOSED, EGO FEELS OBLIGED TO CONTINUE WITH
HER SEXY DANCING, EVEN THOUGH HER HEART'S NOT
IN IT. ANGRY WITH APPETITE FOR ABANDONING HER,
SHE DEFIANTLY DANCES EVEN MORE AGGRESSIVELY,
BEFORE AWKWARDLY LETTING IT PETER OUT.***

FEMALE GENITALS ARE GROSS

SCENE 7. *A house party. EGO & APPETITE are about fourteen. EGO is dancing awkwardly, subtly echoing some of the sexy moves from Dance 3. She speaks to Jack:*

EGO:	APPETITE:
Cool party.	*moves towards Jack*
I love your house.	*hungry, salivating*
So, did you get anything good for your birthday?	

JACK: (Laughing.) "Yeah, I got a blowjob off Stacey! It was awesome."

EGO:	APPETITE:
(Unsure if he's joking, trying to be cool.) Oh yeah? Did you return the favour then?	*shrinks away from JACK, the BOYS and EGO during the following*

JACK: "Ugh. No way. I'm not putting my face in some girl's fishy minge!"

BOY 1: "Yeah, gross!"

BOY 2: "Hairy fish pie? No thanks!"

BOY 1: "I heard Stacey's is like a badly packed kebab!"

BOY 3: "She's had so much dick, I bet it's as baggy as a wizard's sleeve down there!"

EGO LAUGHS AWKWARDLY. HATS ON.

CLITORIS: 'As baggy as a wizard's sleeve'? I don't get it.

BRAIN: Well the idea is that if a girl's had a lot of sex, then her vagina'll stretch and get looser. And wizards have those big baggy sleeves...

CLITORIS: Is that true?

BRAIN: Yeah, they wear those big kaftan things / don't they?

CLITORIS: No – do vaginas really get looser from too much sex?

BRAIN: Oh, no – I don't think so. Vaginas must be quite elastic, because a human baby barely stretches them, and penises are definitely smaller than babies.

CLITORIS: Why did they say that then?

BRAIN: It's a joke.

CLITORIS: Oh. Do you think it's funny?

BRAIN: No, not particularly.

CLITORIS: Why did you laugh?

BRAIN: I want to be cool.

CLITORIS: Oh.

Do you think I'm gross?

BRAIN: No.

CLITORIS: Do I repulse you?

Do I repulse you?

(CLITORIS removes her hat.)

Do I repulse you?

APPETITE, leonine, sniffs at BRAIN/EGO, tries to nuzzle her. Uncomfortable, BRAIN/EGO pushes her away. APPETITE swipes the BRAIN hat off her head and onto the ground. She is now EGO. Angry, EGO walks away.

SEXUAL DESIRE IN WOMEN IS DIRTY

APPETITE pursues her. EGO repeatedly pushes/kicks her away. This transitions into:

DANCE 4 – *EGO STANDS STILL. APPETITE IS BEHIND EGO, HER HANDS EMERGE BETWEEN EGO'S THIGHS IN SLOW, SENSUAL MOVEMENTS, EGO RESISTS TO AVOID BEING OVERCOME WITH DESIRE. APPETITE'S HEAD AND SHOULDERS EMERGE FROM BETWEEN EGO'S THIGHS. EGO PUSHES HER DOWN, ENDS UP SQUATTING OVER HER. APPETITE'S HANDS REACH UP TOWARDS EGO'S FACE IN SENSUAL MOVEMENTS. EGO FORCES THEM DOWN, PUSHES APPETITE BACK THROUGH HER LEGS, AND STANDS, COMPOSING HERSELF. APPETITE STANDS BEHIND EGO. HER HAND REACHES AROUND EGO'S WAIST, CAUSING EGO TO YIELD SLIGHTLY. APPETITE'S ARMS FLICKER AROUND EGO, CAUSING HER TO SHUDDER. TEMPO INCREASES. APPETITE BURSTS OUT BETWEEN EGO'S THIGHS, THRUSTING FORWARD. EGO TRIES TO HOLD HER DOWN, RESULTING IN EGO CROUCHING OVER APPETITE AS SHE LIES ON THE GROUND, AND THE TWO PULSING UP AND DOWN TOGETHER – APPETITE REARING UP AND EGO PUSHING HER DOWN. APPETITE MAKES CHOKING SOUNDS AS EGO PUSHES HER HEAD DOWN. APPETITE BITES EGO'S HAND. THEY MAKE EYE CONTACT: A MOMENT OF REALISATION – THEY DON'T WANT TO KILL EACH OTHER. THEY SEPARATE.*

**GOOD GIRLS DON'T WANT TO HAVE SEX
IF YOU WANT SEX, YOU'RE A SLUT**

SCENE 8. *Hats on. BRAIN & CLITORIS are about sixteen. BRAIN is reading a women's magazine.*

CLITORIS: *(Desperate to know.)* What's an orgasm?

BRAIN: It's like an explosion in your genitals that happens when you have sex.

CLITORIS: *(Worried.)* An explosion?

BRAIN: Yes, a bit like a massive sneeze, but much better. Apparently, a sneeze is an eighth of an orgasm. So, it's eight times more satisfying than a sneeze.

CLITORIS: So, it's a good explosion?

BRAIN: Yes.

CLITORIS: Like fireworks?

BRAIN: Kind of, yes.

CLITORIS: And it happens when you have sex?

BRAIN: Yes.

CLITORIS: LET'S HAVE SEX RIGHT NOW.

BRAIN: What? No, we can't.

CLITORIS: Why not?!

BRAIN: There's no one here to have sex with!

CLITORIS: *(Frustrated.)* Ugh! I REALLY want an orgasm.

Beat.

　　(Inspired.) Let's find someone!

BRAIN: What?

CLITORIS: Let's find someone to have sex with!

CLITORIS approaches members of the audience, propositioning them; 'Do you want some fireworks?', 'Shall we do an orgasm?' etc. BRAIN interjects.

BRAIN: No! Not yet. I don't want to get a reputation.

CLITORIS: A reputation for what?

BRAIN: For being a slut.

CLITORIS: What's a slut?

BRAIN: A girl who has a lot of sex.

CLITORIS: But we haven't had ANY sex.

BRAIN: Alright, a girl who's gagging for it.

CLITORIS: What does that mean?

BRAIN: Well up for it; a bad girl; someone you wouldn't take home to meet your mum; who's a bit dirty.

CLITORIS: We're not dirty.

BRAIN: Exactly – I'm a good girl.

CLITORIS: We're very clean.

BRAIN: I'm a virgin, and I'm not ashamed of it.

CLITORIS: We shower every day.

BRAIN: I don't know why people make such a big deal out of sex.

CLITORIS: We can have a shower now, if you like.

BRAIN: There's a lot more to life than sex.

CLITORIS: I like showers.

BRAIN: I'm not a sex object.

CLITORIS: They're lush.

BRAIN: I am a person.

CLITORIS: All that hot steam.

BRAIN: I am a very intelligent person.

CLITORIS: The warm water running over me.

BRAIN: I have a lot more to offer the world than a good rack, thank you very much.

CLITORIS: Gently caressing me.

BRAIN: I can be really quite insightful, actually.

CLITORIS: Trickling down my shaft.

BRAIN: The mind is far more impressive than the body.

CLITORIS: Teasing me.

BRAIN: Don't look at me like I'm a piece of meat, d'you know what I mean?

CLITORIS: I feel myself rise towards the water.

BRAIN: It's degrading.

CLITORIS: Each tiny stream of hot liquid hits me like a burning needle.

BRAIN: The best form of stimulation is intellectual stimulation.

CLITORIS: I'm pulsing in time with the jets.

BRAIN: Basic, physical urges are a distraction-

CLITORIS: The water undulates over me

BRAIN: a distraction–

CLITORIS: Waves of pleasure cascade through me

BRAIN: What is that?

CLITORIS: I don't know, but it feels good

BRAIN: I'm not sure about this

CLITORIS: I am so sure about this

BRAIN: Is this bad?

CLITORIS: It's wonderful

BRAIN: But is it dirty?

CLITORIS: We're in the shower!

BRAIN: Yes. Yes, okay. I'm just washing myself. That's okay.

CLITORIS: Mmmmmyes

BRAIN: I'm not dirty

CLITORIS: nnnnggggno

BRAIN: I'm clean

CLITORIS: aaahhhhhaah

BRAIN: I'm good and clean

CLITORIS: Oooohooo

BRAIN: Oh God

CLITORIS: whoaohaoohooo

BRAIN: Oh fuck everything's slipping away

CLITORIS: Yes

BRAIN: I can't– I can't–

CLITORIS: Oh yes

BRAIN: Shit what's happening to me?

CLITORIS: Whatever it is, it's spectacular

BRAIN: Are we flying?

CLITORIS: Yes

BRAIN: I feel like I'm melting

CLITORIS: Mmmmmmmnnngggmm

BRAIN: I can't hear anything

CLITORIS: *laughs joyously*

BRAIN: I can't see. I've gone blind.

CLITORIS: Hhhooooaaa

BRAIN: What's happening?

CLITORIS: I don't know. I don't know

BRAIN: Where I am going, but I am going

CLITORIS: I am driving, flying, soaring

BRAIN: My body is carrying me, leading me, controlling me

CLITORIS: I am aching I am throbbing

BRAIN: My whole being is thrumming in time with you

CLITORIS: I am an ocean, swelling, roiling

BRAIN: I am quaking shaking drumming like rain pounding the land

CLITORIS: I am pounding swirling swimming floating breathing

BRAIN: Gasping

CLITORIS: Growing

BRAIN: Flowing

CLITORIS: Oh

BRAIN: Oh

C & B: *long low animalistic sound*

BRAIN: *juddering*

CLITORIS: *juddering*

BRAIN: *heavy breathing*

CLITORIS: *heavy breathing*

Hats off.

IF YOU DON'T HAVE SEX, YOU'RE FRIGID
DON'T BE FRIGID

SCENE 9. *A playground. EGO and APPETITE are about seventeen here. EGO is sitting on a swing. APPETITE is post-coital, her breath heavy, sprawled wherever she collapsed at the end of the previous scene. EGO is talking to a friend.*

EGO:	APPETITE:
I need to have sex.	mm mmmmmm
Not right now, but soon. Very soon. I'm one of the last girls in my year to do it. People are starting to call me frigid. Everyone else is at it like rabbits. Even Becky. I mean, if Becky can get laid, I definitely can. Apparently, it feels amazing.	*laughing with pleasure*

I think I should do it tonight, at the party. It's the perfect opportunity. Everyone'll be there. And I can't leave it much longer, or I'll still be a virgin when I go to uni.

Oh God, that would be awful. All these really cool, sexy, mature types, just like, casually having one-night stands all over the place, and then me being some awkward virgin loser? Can you imagine?

And there's like a 50% chance you'll meet your life partner at uni, so if I fuck it up because I'm shit at sex, I'll basically ruin my life forever.

No, I need to have as much sex as I can between now and then, so that by the time I arrive, I'll be the best shag they've ever had.

hhhmmmm hmm

gently laughing

Right, I've got to look fucking amazing for this party. I'd better start getting ready. I really need a shower.

SEX IS FOR MEN
THE FEMALE ORGASM IS A BONUS

SCENE 10. *Hats on. BRAIN and CLITORIS are about eighteen here.*

BRAIN: We lost our virginity!

CLITORIS: OH NO

BRAIN: It's a good thing!

CLITORIS: But it's so precious!

BRAIN: Not any more – it's just embarrassing after a while.

CLITORIS: Oh.

BRAIN: We're cool now, because we've had sex.

CLITORIS: Are you sure?

BRAIN: Yes!

CLITORIS: We've had sex?!

BRAIN: Yes!

CLITORIS: Has it finished?

BRAIN: Yes.

CLITORIS: *(Devastated.)* Oh.

BRAIN: What?

CLITORIS: *(On the brink of tears.)* I think I missed it.

BRAIN: What?

CLITORIS: I think I missed the sex.

BRAIN: You didn't miss it.

CLITORIS: But I didn't have the whoosh ts ts ping ping pow pow BOOM bbrrrrooooooaaaghwaaooowaaa!

BRAIN: What?!

CLITORIS: The fireworks! Where were the fireworks?

BRAIN: What are you talking about?

CLITORIS: The good explosion?

BRAIN: Oh.

  Well, the girl doesn't always have an orgasm.

CLITORIS: Oh.

  You said that was what sex was for.

BRAIN: It's also to make your partner happy.

CLITORIS: Oh.

BRAIN: Which we did!

CLITORIS: We did?

BRAIN: Yes!

CLITORIS: Did they get an orgasm?

BRAIN: Yes! We gave them one!

CLITORIS: But we didn't get one.

BRAIN: No.

CLITORIS: Why not?

BRAIN: It can be difficult for women to orgasm.

CLITORIS: Why?

BRAIN: It's all a bit complicated. No one's sure exactly how it works.

CLITORIS: I feel like I need to be included. Why didn't you invite me?

BRAIN: I did, but you're famously hard to find.

CLITORIS: I'm right here! Let's try again now.

BRAIN: We can't just ask to try again.

CLITORIS: Why not?

BRAIN: It would be rude.

CLITORIS: Why?

BRAIN: Because it would imply the first time wasn't good enough.

CLITORIS: It *wasn't* good enough. I didn't even know it was happening!

BRAIN: But you can't say that! It would upset them.

CLITORIS: Let's try with someone else then.

CLITORIS begins to proposition members of the audience, 'Can you do the fireworks?', 'You can see me, can't you?' etc.

BRAIN: Stop it! You can't just proposition / strangers!

CLITORIS: I WANT MY EXPLOSION!

APPETITE as a lioness, stalking EGO. EGO is afraid. Magnetically drawn to her, but genuinely terrified she might eat her alive. APPETITE's breath is close to a growl. EGO's breath gets faster and faster. Palpable sexual tension.

**DON'T BE WEIRD
OR SWEATY
OR FLABBY
BE NORMAL
BUT DON'T WEAR NORMAL UNDERWEAR**

SCENE 11. *A student room of a potential sexual partner. BRAIN and CLITORIS are about twenty-one.*

BRAIN: Oh hello.

CLITORIS: Mmmmmm patchouli earthy musky sweet green purple delicious warm oaky sky bright dark soft smush

BRAIN: You smell nice.

CLITORIS: Mmmmm biscuity freckly springy cake fresh from the oven warm on my palm soft melting buttery beneath brushing fingers

BRAIN: Wow, you have really soft hands.

CLITORIS: Lips skin neck shadow nuzzle taste salty taste fruity I want to taste your face can I taste it?

BRAIN: What?

CLITORIS: I want to lick the face – little, light flick of tongue along the jaw line

BRAIN: What?

CLITORIS: I want tongue on bone lingering tickling teeth tasting biting bone

BRAIN: No!

CLITORIS: I want to gently take the bottom lip between teeth suck savour saliva

BRAIN: Ssshh! You're distracting me!

CLITORIS: Run my tongue around the curve of the nose

BRAIN: I need to be sexy in a normal way!

CLITORIS: Trace the nostrils

BRAIN: That is not normal! I need to concentrate.

Okay. Play with your hair, classic.

CLITORIS: Suck the earlobe

BRAIN: Oh, fucking frizz city. Very sexy.

CLITORIS: Eat the whole head

BRAIN: Shut up you freak!
Come on, think. Touch your face, sensually.

CLITORIS: devour the face

BRAIN: Shit, is that a spot?

CLITORIS: nibble the shoulders

BRAIN: Stop being weird.

CLITORIS: Mmmm musky armpit

BRAIN: Oh, no. Now I'm sweating.

CLITORIS: Furry blurry mossy

BRAIN: Has the sweat gone through my top?

CLITORIS: I want to bury my face in armpit

BRAIN: Have I got sweat patches?

CLITORIS: Breathe in steamy scent tangy taste

BRAIN: Oh God, don't come closer, I'm all gross.

CLITORIS: I want to climb inside you

BRAIN: Are you going to kiss me?

CLITORIS: I want my face inside your face

BRAIN: You're going to kiss me.

CLITORIS: Ooooaaagggghhhh electric fizzing sparking
burning fire licking me flicking up legs inside me up my
spine skull vibrating pulsating

BRAIN: That was nice.

CLITORIS: I want to envelop you with pulsing squeezing
bloodflushed fleshy muscle

BRAIN: Okaaay, your hand's moving down my back and
contact with muffin top is imminent – evasive action
required!

CLITORIS: I want your skin to blur blend melt into my skin

BRAIN: Quick! Take your top off!

CLITORIS: Yes!

BRAIN: Hold your belly in!

CLITORIS: What?

BRAIN: You can't have that massive, flabby belly sticking out;
hold it in!

CLITORIS: It's fine; just relax.

BRAIN: Do NOT relax. If you clench your stomach muscles
enough it might look like you're toned.

CLITORIS: But –

BRAIN: Damn! This is a comfy bra, not a sexy bra! I was not
prepared for this.

CLITORIS: Who cares about / the bra?

BRAIN: And the knickers don't match.

CLITORIS: Then take them off!

BRAIN: I can't.

CLITORIS: Oh my / God.

BRAIN: I haven't waxed.

CLITORIS/APPETITE: *(Removing her hat.)* OH, SHUT UP!

BRAIN: What?

CLITORIS/APPETITE: Shut up!

BRAIN: Don't tell me to shut up.

CLITORIS/APPETITE: You're always getting in the way!

BRAIN: In the way of what?!

CLITORIS/APPETITE: FUN! Joy, pleasure, magic,
    delicious sensations, physical connections / emotional
    transformations

BRAIN: What are you talking about?

CLITORIS/APPETITE: Sex! You're RUINING SEX. You're
    making sex BAD.

BRAIN/EGO: *(Removing her hat.)* Maybe sex is bad.

BRAIN/EGO turns to read the projections:

SEX IS SEEDY
ORAL SEX IS PARTICULARLY FILTHY

SCENE 12. *Playground. EGO is on the swing, speaking to a friend.*
APPETITE is at a distance, shrunken and very quiet. EGO and APPETITE
are early twenties here.

EGO:	APPETITE:
Don't get me wrong, I enjoy sex,	
I do, I have a lovely time while it's happening.	*hopeful*
I just prefer not to think about what is happening, specifically.	*disappointed, confused*
I enjoy how it feels	*smiles in agreement*
but without engaging with the practicalities of what's	
actually going on down there. I mean, I know	*looks to EGO, questioning*
I need clitoral stimulation to come,	*nods with pleasure*
but I'm vague on the details. I've only really used a pillow, or the shower or something on myself, so I've got no idea what my lover actually does with	
their hands or tongue or whatever. And in the heat of the moment it's fine, but if I stop to think about the mechanics of it when I'm not already aroused, like now, I get a tiny bit embarrassed and grossed out. Is that really bad?	*shrugs shoulders – does it matter, if it feels good?*
	upset, tearing up

It's a bit like a meat eater
who loves animals – when
they're eating bacon, they
don't think about where it   *confused*
came from, they just enjoy
the taste, the smell, the
crispiness on their tongue…   *smiles*
they don't think about the
pig, as intelligent as their
pet dog, squealing with
fear as it's dragged to be
slaughtered. But when there   *horrified*
isn't any bacon lulling their
senses and distracting them,
if they think about the pig's
throat being cut then, and
imagine the blood pouring
out, then they might feel   *begins to cry*
kind of grossed out and
maybe a bit ashamed of
eating the bacon. Y'know?

awkward pause

                                stops crying

No? Never mind, I didn't
mean– just ignore me. I love
sex. Sex is great. People say
I'm sexy. I like that. I like   *begins moving her body, shaking*
being sexy. I like the feeling   *off the rejection and channelling*
of being desired. Y'know,   *her positive sexual energy in a*
when you can tell someone's   *way that becomes dancing*
looking at you – lusting after
you? I love that.

EGO clocks APPETITE's dancing. Stands. Reads the projections.

SEXINESS IS EMPOWERING
SEX IS A PERFORMANCE

DANCE 5 – APPETITE DOES WILD, FREE DANCING,
GROUNDED IN THE EARTH. EGO REPEATS A 'SEXY'
POSE FROM DANCE 3 AND TAKES IT FURTHER, GOING
INTO A SLIGHTLY AGGRESSIVE 'SEXY' ROUTINE –
ARMS RAISED ABOVE HEAD WITH WRISTS CROSSED,
HIPS CIRCLING. EGO CLOCKS APPETITE AND TRIES
TO INCLUDE HER/CONTROL HER, BY SHOWING
HER HOW TO DO THE 'SEXY' MOVES. APPETITE
CONTINUES HER JOYOUS, UNINHIBITED MOVEMENTS.
FRUSTRATED, EGO MOVES APPETITE'S ARMS INTO
THE 'CORRECT' POSITION. APPETITE RESISTS,
BUT EGO FORCES HER BODY INTO 'SEXY' SHAPES
AND EVENTUALLY APPETITE SUBMITS, SO THAT IT
FINISHES WITH THE TWO WOMEN DANCING SIDE
BY SIDE, APPETITE GOING THROUGH THE MOTIONS,
HER FACE IMPASSIVE; DEAD BEHIND THE EYES.

APPETITE walks away. EGO reads the projections

SEX OBJECTS DON'T HAVE BODY HAIR
SEX IS A GIFT YOU CAN GIVE
SEX IS BETTER THE MORE ATTRACTIVE YOU ARE
LINGERIE HELPS YOU GET IN THE MOOD
SPECIAL OCCASIONS = GREAT SEX

SCENE 13. *Home shared with partner. EGO and APPETITE are about thirty.*

EGO: APPETITE:
A little too self-aware, performing

It's your birthday.
I'm getting ready to surprise
you.
I trim my unruly bush until
it's as neat as Centre Court
at Wimbledon. But it's still
covering too much ground.
It spreads as far as my
thighs. Thighs are no place
for pubes. I spread warm
wax onto my groin.
It feels lovely, like a hot flannel.

                               mmmmmmmmmmm

Then I rip it off. It feels less
lovely.
                              sharp intakes of breath
Like a thousand burning
needles piercing into me.
But now I feel clean. It
doesn't smell as fishy
without the hair. I have a
perfect landing strip.
It makes me feel kinda naughty.   *nnnaughty*
I like it.

                        little laugh

I lay a trail of rose petals
leading to the bedroom. I light
candles and turn on the stereo.   *hums a sexy song*
I set a semi-circle of
beautifully wrapped presents
on the bed and then I
artfully arrange myself at
their centre:

the greatest gift of them all.
I'm tied up with ribbons;
a black silky bow atop my
bottom at the base of a lacy
basque, the soft mounds of
my bosom presented like
mouth-watering delicacies
on a silver platter.

soft mounds
mmmmmmmmm mmmmm
licks her lips

Your jaw hits the floor. You
can't believe your luck.
You're so hungry for me.
I look fucking amazing.
I am sex incarnate. I feel like
a Beyoncé video come to
vivid, voracious life.
Looking down at myself is
making my clit hard. The
sound of my own groans turns
me on even more. I watch my
body writhe. It's like having
HD porn streamed straight to
my eyeballs.
Fuck me, I'm hot.

hhhhuunnnngry

sssssexxxxxx
vvvvvvivid vvvoraaaciousss

groaning with pleasure

h h hhooot hothothothothot

this is a bit forced, now
The following year, I buy
new lingerie, and again I
wrap myself up in it. Again,
I paint my face to look like
the face of a sexy woman.

tired, now, and gradually
becoming more numb

I am a sexy woman.

This time I shave my pubes
instead of waxing.

I'm still a very sexy woman.

As I perch on the bed, I
catch sight of myself in the
mirror: I look like a stranger.
When you walk in, I shrink
a little.

Your eyes rove over the
curves, salivating.

I feel like I'm underwater.

Your gaze stops at the
surface of my skin.

But I'm swimming
somewhere below the surface.

Do you see me? You see a
sexy woman. But is that me?

I'm in here.

I'm in here; can you see me?

Do you see me?

I'm in here

I'm in here; can you see me?

Do you see me? I'm in here.

I'm in here.

Can you see you me?

I sink deeper. I'm floating in
the shadowy recesses near
the sea floor.

Quiet and invisible. A cool
numbness ripples through
me.

Quiet and invisible. A cool
numbness ripples through me.

*APPETITE as a lioness – she is weakened; starving hungry. She makes
a pathetic attempt to make contact with EGO, but EGO instinctively
moves away, and APPETITE collapses on the ground at her feet. EGO
looks at her. Takes a moment, perhaps touches her, perturbed. Her turn
away transitions into:*

SCENE 1 part 2. *Bedroom shared with partner. EGO and APPETITE are early thirties here. APPETITE is weak and small, in a position echoing their positions at the end of DANCE 4 and foreshadowing the collapse in DANCE 6.*

EGO: APPETITE:

I'm sorry. I don't know why
I find this so difficult to talk
about. I feel really – I feel a bit
pressured, a bit under pressure
and I don't know – I do,
I really enjoy it when we have   *weakly hopeful moaning*
sex. Whenever we have sex,   *and sighing*
it's great, like I come pretty
much every time, you always
make sure I've come before
you do, you're very attentive,
and it's great.

I just, I guess my sex drive   *the sighs become quietly*
just isn't as big as yours. I   *despairing*
don't have, like, an appetite
that needs sating. I don't
really notice if we don't do
it for ages. Or, I do because
I'm worried that you'll be
frustrated, but physically, I
don't miss it. Like that's why   *lost, tearful*
I don't masturbate, really,
because it's not like an urge
that I have that needs an
outlet. I can go for however
long, and it's not a problem.

It's more of a problem for me to
go without intimacy, like if we
didn't hug for a week, I would
really feel that –
I want that closeness; that
contact, the kissing, y'know?
But it doesn't particularly need   *gasping and gulping for air*
to be sexual for me. I mean, I
wouldn't want to never have
sex again, but – I don't know.   *giving up and collapsing*
I'm sorry.

SCENE 14. *Bedroom shared with partner. EGO and APPETITE are early thirties.*

***DANCE 6 – INTERCUT WITH SCENE – APPETITE IS
INANIMATE/FLOPPY/EXHAUSTED, EGO IS TRYING TO GET
HER TO MOVE/DANCE/BECOME AROUSED. EGO DANCES
GENTLY & SENSUOUSLY, STROKES APPETITE'S BACK.***

EGO: Hey… It's sexy time! Your favourite time! Time to do
your thing!

*EGO ROLLS APPETITE, LIFTS HER TO STANDING BY
THE ARMS. APPETITE BUCKLES AT THE KNEES, EGO
CATCHES HER AND PUTS HER ARM AROUND HER NECK.*

EGO: Come on, it's been over a month since we last had sex.
That's too long.

*EGO TRIES TO WALTZ WITH APPETITE, BUT HER NECK
KEEPS LOLLING BACK. APPETITE COLLAPSES TO THE
FLOOR IN A WATERY MOVEMENT. EGO LIFTS HER
UPPER BODY, WAVING HER ARMS.*

EGO: Please, people in successful relationships have sex at least twice a week. I read a survey.

If you don't have sex with someone, you can't expect them not to cheat on you. And I really don't want to be cheated on.

APPETITE FALLS TO THE FLOOR COMPLETELY, EGO TRIES TO LIFT HER, CRADLING HER HEAD, THEN GENTLY SLAPPING HER CHEEK TO ROUSE HER – INCREASINGLY DESPERATE. APPETITE BRIEFLY SEEMS TO REVIVE, BUT THEN COLLAPSES AND CURLS UP ON THE GROUND. EGO SHAKES HER WITH INCREASING VIOLENCE, THEN MOVES AWAY.

EGO: Oh, you're fucking useless, aren't you?! When I want you to be quiet, you won't leave me alone, and now I actually need you, nothing! What's wrong with you?

Pause.

Please. I need to have sex tonight for the sake of my relationship, and I can't do it without you. I need you.

APPETITE SLOWLY DRAGS HERSELF TO STANDING, LEONINE. EGO TRIES TO FORCE APPETITE INTO SEXY POSES FROM DANCE 5, BUT SHE FIGHTS BACK. EGO & APPETITE FIGHT. APPETITE ENDS UP RESTRAINED, ON THE FLOOR, FROM WHERE SHE SPEAKS.

Partway through the following speech, APPETITE/ACTOR rips her clothes off, as if escaping from bonds, and ends up completely naked, and free.

APPETITE/ACTOR:
Let me out! Fucking let me out. I can't breathe. You're choking me. I'm suffocating. I'm drowning in your shame. Stop trying to hide me, quash me, squash me, bury me. Coward. Weak, pathetic, conformist coward! You can bury me in the shadows of your mind, soiling me with your

thoughts, but I am a seed; I will grow. I will outgrow you, with your desperate need for approval. I don't need your approval, I don't want your approval, I don't give a shitting fuck what you think! You can't kill me. I'm growing, I'm expanding, stretching, your insides are shattering because I'm too big. I'm too big for this cage you've hidden me in. I'm too big for you to contain. You are breaking, splintering, creaking under the weight of me – the giant, expanding, expansive weight of what I am and what I can be and what I can feel. Fuck your thoughts. I can feel thunder in my loins. I can feel rumbling, climbing, growling up through me from my roots, up, up, up. I can feel myself stretching, cracking you open, smashing through the yoke of your fragility, your fear, your rules, your judgement. I am coming, I am coming faster than you can see, faster than you can think, faster than you can stop me. You cannot stop me. I will not be stopped. I will not be held down. I will not be silenced. I will not be shamed. I am bigger than you. I am bigger than all of you! I am not a product to be neatly packaged, I am not a plastic doll to be cooed over, I am not here to be pretty or nice, or sexy. I will not please you. I will not reduce myself to a fraction of my size and power and immensity to protect you, I will not shrink myself to fit into your ideals. I will not contort myself any longer to conform to your expectations; your expectations will be exceeded. I will exceed you. I will exceed the limitations set down. I will burn you to the ground. Don't tell me to be quiet! Don't shush me, like a baby. I am not your baby. I *make* babies. I make life! I take the shit and the shame, and the murky shadows of your disgust and I bring forth life. From my insides bursts a blinding brightness that obliterates all else and soars through the senses and cuts to the core. Unashamed, unabashed, unsoiled, unfettered, wide-throated, howling LIFE. I am a woman and I will be heard. I will be heard above the din of your insecurity and your need to fit in. I have needs of my own. I need. I want. I hunger. I thirst. I crave. And I will eat. I will roar, and I will feed. I will climb out of this skin. I will shed it like a snake, and I will uncoil my knot of muscle, and I will be free. I cannot be contained by your tiny mind. I will not be the object of your gaze, or the object of your lust, or the object of your affection. I am not an object. I am a goddess. I will live for you no more. I will live for me. In the fullness of my ardour, my ambition, my hunger, my drive, my rage. I will live in the light in the heat of the flames of my own desire, and fuck you. I am me, and I will live, so fuck you.

Pause.

EGO/WRITER: What the fuck's going on? Who are you?

APPETITE/ACTOR: I'm you.

EGO/WRITER: But you just said 'fuck you' to me.

APPETITE/ACTOR: Well you also sort of embody the patriarchy for me right now.

EGO/WRITER: What? You can't make me the patriarchy! I'm not the patriarchy, I'm a woman!

APPETITE/ACTOR: Well, you've been shovelling a fuck of a lot of patriarchal bullshit onto me. You pretty much buried me in it.

EGO/WRITER: You being *me*?

APPETITE/ACTOR: Yes, part of you – I'm playing your clitoris, aren't I? Or maybe not literally your clitoris, but, y'know, your sexual appetite. Your metaphorical clitoris.

EGO/WRITER: Right. I didn't envisage my metaphorical clitoris being so… angry.

APPETITE/ACTOR: Oh, I'm sorry. Should I just keep waiting, patiently and quietly, like a good little girl, until you've quashed every drop of life out of me?

51

EGO/WRITER: Alright, bloody hell, I'm not the enemy, here. I'm you, apparently. If we're the same person, surely we ought to be on the same team?

APPETITE/ACTOR: Exactly! So why do you constantly push me down? Why do you suppress your own sexuality?

EGO/WRITER: I don't! I've done so many things to try and be sexy! I've got all the fucking lingerie, the expensive perfume, I eat well and try and stay in shape so I look good in it, I taught myself how to pluck my eyebrows and apply make-up properly, because my mum didn't do any of that, I shaved my armpits, I waxed my pubes – that really fucking hurt, because I've got fucking hench pubes, and every single one leaves a little spot of blood where it's been ripped out. I am awesome at sexy dancing, I know I've never used sex toys, but the whole things just feels a bit plastic, but maybe I'm being narrow-minded – I'll give it a go / lots of people have told me vibrators are amazing –

APPETITE/ACTOR: I don't care about any of that.

EGO/WRITER: What?

APPETITE/ACTOR: That means nothing to me. I don't care what you look like. That's not what sexuality is. Do you think there was no sexual energy before lingerie was invented? When people just walked around unaware of the hot stink of their sweat? Before tweezers and mascara and lipstick and razors, do you think there was no beauty, no lust, no throbbing aching desire? I'm not a recent invention – I am eternal. I have always been here.

Oh shit, I'm going to have to get transcendental on you, aren't I?

EGO/WRITER: What? No, please don't.

APPETITE/ACTOR: Yes, I can see I'm going to have to lead everyone in a meditation.

EGO/WRITER: Seriously, you're going to do naked meditation? You realise you're going to become a parody of yourself?

APPETITE/ACTOR: *(Serenely.)* You've left me with no choice.

EGO/WRITER: Oh no, not the meditation voice, please.

APPETITE/ACTOR: Oh yes, it's coming.

EGO/WRITER: *(To audience.)* I'm sorry.

(APPETITE/ACTOR's voice starts off parodying a stereotypical guided meditation tone, but gradually becomes more natural.)

APPETITE/ACTOR: Please make sure you are sitting comfortably, your feet flat on the ground, your hands resting on your thighs, palms facing heavenward, and your eyes closed. *(To EGO/WRITER.)* DO IT.

(EGO/WRITER obeys.)

Turn back, travel through time beyond comprehension. Days and nights dizzyingly vast in number, until you land, 5,000 years ago, in Mesopotamia; land between rivers. Before it became Iraq, Kuwait, Syria, Turkey. The universe is a closed dome surrounded by a primordial saltwater sea. The Earth a plain, swimming on water. Over this is arched the solid vault of heaven. To this vault are fastened the lights, the stars.

You are Innana, goddess of love, fertility, sex. Your people call you 'Queen of Heaven'. Listen: voices raised in song: breath, pushed up from believing bellies praises your lap of honey. Notes of joy give thanks for the bounty that pours forth from your womb. Your sexuality is the earth's fertility. Lettuces are lovingly described as your pubic hair. Your worshippers carve your courage into stone; you are riding a roaring lioness. Your vulva is a sacred site. It is written: 'her vulva was wondrous to behold / Rejoicing at her wondrous vulva, the young woman applauded herself'. You see your velvety folds of flesh flowering between your thighs and you swell with pride.

(To EGO.) You feel your sexual power and you rejoice. Because you are her.

EGO/WRITER: She sounds awesome. But I'm not her. I *wish* I could be like her. So delighted with her genitals that she literally applauds herself! Clearly no one ever called her fanny a hairy fish pie!

APPETITE/ACTOR: You can be her. You are her. You just have to listen to me. You haven't been listening.

EGO/WRITER: I'm sorry; I don't know what you're saying.

APPETITE/ACTOR: I'm saying, what might happen, if you trust your senses? If you follow your nose, and your fingertips, and your breath?

EGO/WRITER: I don't know what that means.

APPETITE/ACTOR: It means, how would it be if you stopped looking at yourself? If you turned off the spotlight? How would it feel to stop searching for your own reflection in the eyes of others? What if you stopped trying to impress them? Stopped craving their approval? Stopped judging yourself?

EGO/WRITER: That's impossible.

APPETITE/ACTOR: Maybe. Would you like to try?

EGO/WRITER takes a big breath in. She looks at the audience. Looks at APPETITE/ACTOR. Stands. Slowly looks around at everyone in the audience. Silence. Looks back at APPETITE/ACTOR. Looks down. Slows her breathing. Deliberately turns her back on the audience. Centres herself. Removes her clothes, one item at a time, as she walks steadily upstage, away from the audience. When she is naked, she crouches down and splashes her face and body with water, cleansing herself. She relaxes physically. She turns towards the audience, stands, and lifts her head to face them.

*DANCE 7 – EGO TRIES TO WALK PROUDLY TOWARDS THE
AUDIENCE, BUT QUITE QUICKLY CONTORTS INTO THE
SHAME PHYSICALITY FROM BEFORE. SHE STRUGGLES TO
OVERCOME THIS WITH 'SEXY' POSES, AS IN DANCE 3. AT
THIS POINT, APPETITE APPROACHES, PRESSES HER NAKED
BODY INTO EGO'S SIDE, AND ECHOES THE MOVEMENTS
FROM DANCE 1: GENTLY TAKES HER HAND, AND PLACES
IT ON HER CHEEK, ENCOURAGING HER TO SWAY SLOWLY.
EGO ATTEMPTS TO INCORPORATE THIS INTO A SEXY
MOVEMENT. APPETITE GENTLY TAKES BOTH EGO'S ARMS,
WRAPS THEM AROUND HER, AND PLACES HER HANDS
ON HER BELLY. EGO RELAXES INTO IT, GIVING APPETITE
HER WEIGHT AND SWAYING IN TIME WITH HER. APPETITE
TAKES EGO'S WEIGHT, BENDS FORWARD, SWINGS FROM
SIDE TO SIDE, STEPS FORWARD, CROUCHING DOWN,
WHILE MANTAINING FULL BODY CONTACT. THEY SIT ON
THE FLOOR, ARMS AROUND EACH OTHER, HEADS BURIED
IN NECKS, CIRCLING FROM THE WAIST. MOVING OUT OF
THIS, APPETITE LIFTS EGO'S HAND UP INTO THE AIR, AND
THEY BOTH FOLLOW THE IMPULSE UP TO STANDING.
APPETITE STANDS BEHND EGO. SHE LIFTS HER ARMS,
PLACES HER HANDS ON EGO'S BELLY – EGO'S HANDS REST
ON TOP. PLACES HER HANDS ON EGO'S CHEST – EGO'S
HANDS REST ON TOP. FINALLY, APPETITE LIFTS HER ARMS,
SO BOTH WOMEN HAVE THEIR ARMS RAISED UP
AND SPREAD OUT WIDE, LIKE WINGS.*

*Pause. EGO/WRITER takes some time and space to feel this new sensation
of really being in her body and not fighting it. It feels good. Throughout
the following, she is connected to her body and physically free in a way
that she hasn't been up until this point.*

EGO/WRITER: *(To APPETITE/ACTOR.)* I've had a revelation:
I don't care how often I have sex. It doesn't matter to me.
The thought of keeping count makes me feel suffocated.

APPETITE/ACTOR: Yeah?

EGO/WRITER: And trying to conform to some arbitrary beauty standard just makes me feel shit. It's exhausting, it drains the colour from everything. It makes my body a sculpted lump of flesh that doesn't feel like me anymore. The feeling of rejecting that, of saying: I like my body as it is; I like the curls of hair crawling up my belly from my pubes; I like the discharge in my pants; I like to sniff my own armpit; that feeling is like flying. It's like my ribs swinging apart and sprouting wings.

APPETITE/ACTOR: Yes! I don't want to be a sexy doll. I don't want to be thin, and toned and smooth and taut and perfect. I don't want to learn how to please. I want to explore us like we're a planet I've never been to before. I want to savour us like we're a flavour that's just been invented.

EGO/WRITER: Yes! I want to devour. I want to taste, eat, lick, suck, bite. I want to gulp at the air and fill my nostrils with the sharp delicious musk of our stench. I want to grab, grasp, grip flesh, squeeze muscle. I want sweat smeared across skin, dripping from chins.

APPETITE/ACTOR: I want to meet head on. I want to growl with hunger as I sink my teeth in. I want my lover to lap up my sweat and my juice and savour every drop on their tongue. I want to plunge in without being able to see the bottom. I want to thrum with the excitement of unknown depths to discover. I want to get my hands dirty with a stupid great grin on my face. I want to laugh.

EGO/WRITER: I want sex to be earthy, messy, funny, surprising, exhausting. I want to be deeply rooted in myself and to soar above myself at the same time.

APPETITE/ACTOR: I want to want something different every day.

EGO/WRITER: I want. I want. I want.

APPETITE/ACTOR: I am a woman, and I have wants.

And right now, I want to put my clothes back on.

EGO/WRITER: Oh. But, we're kind of using the nudity to make a statement.

APPETITE/ACTOR: My naked body is not a tool for you to utilise in order to make a point. It's my home.

EGO/WRITER: Right, yes.

APPETITE/ACTOR: I get to choose what I do with my body, no one else.

EGO/WRITER: Of course.

APPETITE/ACTOR: If I want to express myself by tearing my clothes off because I feel like I'm suffocating, I will.

EGO/WRITER: Yeah.

APPETITE/ACTOR: And if I want to put my clothes back on because there's a fucking draft and I would be more comfortable in clothes, then I will.

EGO/WRITER: Absolutely. You're right. Sorry.

APPETITE/ACTOR: *(Getting dressed.)* If you want to be naked, that's entirely up to you.

EGO/WRITER: Actually, I'm a bit chilly too. And it feels a bit awkward now we've drawn attention to it like this.

APPETITE/ACTOR: Get dressed then.

EGO/WRITER: But I feel like removing my clothes symbolised shedding the patriarchal values that I'd internalised, so putting them back on might undermine that a bit.

APPETITE/ACTOR: What, like, putting your bra on would imply that you're going to start shaving your armpits again?

EGO/WRITER: Yeah, kind of.

APPETITE/ACTOR: Maybe that's okay.

EGO/WRITER: Really?

APPETITE/ACTOR: Yes. I mean, you're allowed to shave your armpits if you want to. You're allowed to wear make-up, or lingerie, or anything you want.

EGO/WRITER: Even though they're the tools of the systematic oppression of women in our society?

APPETITE/ACTOR: Do you know what the biggest tool of oppression is? Telling women what they can and cannot do. Fuck that. If you choose to conform to some sexist expectations sometimes, that is your choice. To be honest, you probably will, won't you? Maybe because it makes your life a bit easier, or simply because it's fun.

EGO/WRITER: I guess so. I want to be a good feminist though; I don't want to let the side down.

APPETITE/ACTOR: Bloody hell, life's hard enough as it is – let's not use feminism as yet another stick to beat women with and make them feel guilty and inadequate, alright?

EGO/WRITER: Yeah, alright.

EGO/WRITER gets dressed. APPETITE/ACTOR may help her to speed things up.

This is a bit awkward now, though isn't it? Everyone just watching me get dressed.

APPETITE/ACTOR: It's fine, no one's watching. *(To the audience.)* You're not watching, are you? No. I tell you what, it's a bit bright, isn't it? Shall we bring the lights down? Yeah, let's just bring these down a touch.

Lights fade in steps

Lovely – bit more. That's better isn't it? Touch more.
Great – keep going.

Blackout.

Perfect.

EGO/WRITER & APPETITE/ACTOR speak quietly, in the dark.

EGO/WRITER: I'm dressed now.

APPETITE/ACTOR: This is nice, though isn't it? Like being
back in the womb.

EGO/WRITER: Is this what the womb's like?

APPETITE/ACTOR: Mmm, I think so.

Shall we do the ending like this?

EGO/WRITER: Yeah.

MY VULVA IS WONDROUS
MY DESIRE IS VALID
MY BODY IS MY HOME
I AM NOT AN OBJECT
I AM A FUCKING LIONESS

*WRITER and ACTOR begin speaking the following. Gradually their
voices are joined by the voices of more and more women, becoming a
chorus ringing out of the darkness. The other women can be pre-recorded.*

Look – a lioness, caged behind bars, prowling.
Her fur burnished gold softening for you, imagine
Breathing; your nostrils buried, nuzzling, the hairs
Of her coat stroking cheek skin gentle as flame.

No. Stop. Now. Now note how the soil shifts
In place, confettis your feet in awe
Of her roar. Listen –

To your bones judder against the tautness
Of muscle, straining to touch your clammy skin.
Will you run? No. She is caged, and you are safe. You
Can admire the way the whites of her fangs puncture
The sky, slicing out of the bloody cavern opening
Up in her face. You can gasp, your pulse quickening
With excitement. Your skin prickling awake,
Each hair along your spine standing to attention,
A Mexican wave up, up, up from the cleavage of your bottom
To the nape of your neck. Your body thrilling
To the sonorous bass arcing up out of her belly
And into yours.

Feel the vibrations in your gut. The fearsome tremors
Of a beast, caged by your ribs, your skin, your iron will,
Your self-control, your discipline, your femininity, your
conformity.
Feel the cracks start to appear. Can everyone hear your heart
Punching your chest, bruising you from the inside, trying
To escape? Is the rush of blood audible only to you?
It's so loud. Terrifyingly, disorientingly loud.

A rupture.

Lock eyes with the lioness. Hold her amber gaze, even
As your mouth gets hot and dry and sweat bubbles
Through the pores in your face – hold her gaze.
Walk towards her. Keep looking and you will see
Yourself silhouetted against the sun, reflected
In her dilated pupils as she glares unfalteringly back.

Grip the bars of her cage. Feel the cold steel, hard
Against your palms. Now push.
Push harder.
Push.
Push until your arms are wide. Wide open, and the bars

Curve gently, creating an opening like a line drawing of a vulva.
And – oh – oh fuck, this is it. She coils into herself, and springs
Up, her hind legs launching that heaving mass of muscle
Towards you, towards the opening in her cage – such
Power! With all her power she runs and leaps, mouth wide,
out of the opening
Of your vagina. The blood red mouth of your vagina roars
And the lioness soars through the air between your thighs,
And lands, for a split second, on the soil at your feet,
Before her paws are in the air again and she is flying
Free.
Go!
Run, leap, land on her back, her muscles rippling beneath
your feet,
The wind in your face. Adrenaline coursing through you so fast
You feel you will burst out of your skin.
Ride her like a wave.

END

SECOND ACT

In the original production, the scripted portion of the play, which is a performance by two actors, was followed by a second act, which was a conversation with the audience. This was not a traditional post-show discussion, where the audience ask questions of the creatives involved in making the piece; rather it was an opportunity for the audience to reflect on what the play had sparked in them personally. This was an important part of the show, because one of our key aims in making it was to generate further conversation on the themes the play explores.

After a short interval, the audience were welcomed back into the theatre. The playing area had been transformed into a cosier environment, where everyone could sit together. Bella invited everyone to write down any emotions that they had felt whilst watching the performance. These were gathered together, and Bella picked out common words and invited people to share when/why they had felt that thing. She then facilitated an organic discussion arising out of whatever people shared. The focus was on emotional responses, rather than intellectual or critical responses, aimed towards enabling personal insights and cultivating empathy, rather than encouraging debate of any kind. Bella moved from the more challenging emotions, through to the more enjoyable ones, in the hope of striking an optimistic tone.

Bella Heesom

MY WORLD HAS EXPLODED
A LITTLE BIT

OBERON BOOKS
LONDON

WWW.OBERONBOOKS.COM

An **All About You** production.

Premiered at Underbelly, Edinburgh Festival Fringe, 4th August 2016, with the following company:

Bella/Guide/Writer   Bella Heesom
Eva/Assistant/Actor   Sara Alexander*

Director & Dramaturg   Donnacadh O'Briain
Writer & Producer   Bella Heesom
Set & Costume Design   Elizabeth Harper
Composer   Anna O'Grady
Sound & Video Design   Keegan Curran
Lighting Design   Christopher Nairne
Technical Stage Manager   Cassie Harrison
Producer   Matthew Lister
Executive Producer   Mark Fordyce

previously known as Eva Alexander

The play previewed at the Tristan Bates Theatre, London, on 11th August 2015. Esh Alladi played Esh/Assistant/Actor (the character is named after the actor playing it), Stefania Procter was the Stage Manager and Bella Heesom was the sole producer.

THANKS

Donnacadh, for being so generous with your time and energy and believing in me as a writer on very little evidence; for somehow always asking the right questions, and for all of your 'terrible ideas'; this play wouldn't exist without you. Anna, for the beautiful music, and inadvertently inspiring the Assistant character. Esh, for being there for me when everything was falling apart, as an actor, a doctor, and a friend. Liz, for your beautifully evocative drawings. Keegan, for all those hours on Keynote without complaint, and the beautiful clouds moving across windows. Sara, for being so brilliant it forced me to up my game, and for missing your big family holiday to slum it at the Fringe. Michael Rundle, for your support – as a friend and a tech guru. Rebecca Pitt, Louise Calf, Isabelle Schoelcher, Mike Davis. Jack Lowe, Hannah Moss, David Ralfe, Russell Bender. Christopher Nairne, Edward Moore, Max Sobol, Remi Bruno-Smith, Alexandra Anzemberger, Erik Perera, and Nick Goodman. The Yard Theatre.

Matthew, for your love and support, always. Everyone on Team Pete, especially Deb, Maisie, Margaret, Bruce and Andrew. (Thank you for not hating the play or me for writing it.) All my friends who sent kind messages and cards and flowers, especially Charlie and Aaron, for being on the other end of the phone. The NHS, and all the wonderful people who cared for Pete and Yasmin. Mum's loving carers; Jo, Joe-Ann and Gaynor. The carol singers from the hospital, whoever you are. (Yes, that really happened.)

Everyone who donated to the crowd funding campaigns, especially Mark Fordyce, Timothy Chick, Margaret & Bruce Ferne, Craig de Silva, Elaine Richardson, Linda Diotallevi, Lieve Vandenhoeck, Deborah Evans, Judith & Duncan Campbell, Renate Nyborg, Melis Erda, Daniel Pearson, Richard Moross, Samuel Genen, and Maisie Ferne Evans. Everyone who came to see the show and gave me a hug or just looked deeply into my eyes afterwards – thank you for being so open. You made me feel less alone, and I will always treasure those moments of connection.

ALL ABOUT YOU is the creative collaboration between writer/performer Bella Heesom and Olivier Award-winning director/dramaturg Donnacadh O'Briain. Our work is characterised by a playful approach to big themes. We strive to cultivate empathy by exposing our common humanity, in all its raw, flawed fragility and beauty. We create theatre with the audience experience as the central focus, using a flexible fourth wall, and audience interaction. Our plays combine unflinching emotional honesty, intellectual rigour, and a good dose of silliness, to invite audiences to delve deep inside themselves, find the soft, shadowy parts, and explore them with curiosity and kindness.

ALL ABOUT YOU was formed in 2015 following our years of fruitful collaboration as actor and director on a number of diverse projects. *My World Has Exploded A Little Bit* was the first play we made together. The show received audience, critical and industry acclaim at the Edinburgh Festival Fringe 2016, followed by a Highly Commended run at VAULT Festival, and a successful national tour in 2017, supported by Arts Council England. Our second show was *Rejoicing At Her Wondrous Vulva The Young Woman Applauded Herself*, which was commissioned by Ovalhouse, and supported by Arts Council England.

'A genuinely valuable piece of work'
Scotsman

'radical honesty and honest artistry'
★★★★★ *Edinburgh Spotlight*

See **bellaheesom.com** for reviews, production photos, trailers, short films etc.

Bella Heesom in production
Photographer Edward Moore
Artist and Set Designer Elizabeth Harper

Bella Heesom in production
Photographer Edward Moore
Artist and Set Designer Elizabeth Harper

Characters

BELLA / GUIDE / WRITER

EVA / ASSISTANT / ACTOR

Notes on the text:

One performer, the writer, plays three characters, paired with 3 modes of storytelling:

BELLA is Bella in 2010 & 2012. She exists within acted **SCENES** depicting moments from her life, and is unaware of the audience. She does not wear glasses.

GUIDE is a hyper-logical version of present day Bella who is giving a presentation about managing mortality to a group who are attending her lecture. She presents the guide in a series of **STEPS**. Within these, she incorporates the **SCENES** to illustrate her point, like a documentary video clip embedded in a PowerPoint. She is trying to hide the fact that she and BELLA are the same person, hence using her full name: Isobel. She is unaware of the interruptions by WRITER. She wears glasses.

WRITER is the writer performing the play, breaking the fourth wall, interrupting the action, and addressing the audience directly with reference to the content of the play, and her past life experiences. She exists within **STEP-OUTS**. She does not wear glasses.

NB: The distinctions between the three characters become blurred as the play progresses, and collapses completely at the end.

A second actor plays the GUIDE's ASSISTANT. They also play an original piano score, live. Their character name is their real name (in this version: EVA). ASSISTANT wears glasses.

During **SCENES**, the second actor is present as themself (EVA), narrating and/or watching the moments depicted in the scenes as if they are happening in the present moment (no glasses).

During **STEP-OUTS**, the second actor is present as themself (ACTOR) – an actor and pianist, who is performing the play with WRITER (no glasses).

ASSISTANT can be played by a person of any gender.

Text in *italics* is spoken by the second actor (EVA) into a microphone by the piano, except for the opening section, which is spoken by the WRITER into a microphone by the piano.

All underlined text appears on a screen onstage as projected text.

In **SCENES**, it's used for the speech of characters who are not physically represented onstage, e.g. Pete, Doctor etc.

Within **STEPS,** this is used for titles and key points in the Guide, as in a PowerPoint presentation.

Each **STEP** is introduced by a flourish on the piano and announced by GUIDE and/or ASSISTANT.

Text *(in brackets)* is stage directions, and not to be spoken aloud.

For my mum and my dad.
Thank you. I love you.

(As the audience enter the theatre, GUIDE and ASSISTANT are present in the space, welcoming them; shaking hands, suggesting seats etc. The text on the screen onstage reads–)

<u>A Logical, Philosophical Guide To Managing Mortality</u>
<u>(17 Steps to Conquering Death.)</u>

***

SCENE 1
(Sunny residential street, London, early afternoon.)

WRITER:

The sky is wide open. Bright. Not dazzling, just… smiling. The afternoon is rocking back on its heels. A young woman walks through warm currents of air. She feels light, like there's a balloon in the middle of her, gently buoying her every step.

She remembers her dad's email from last night. It's a reply to a one-line message from her, asking how he is. He spends half of it asking how she is. He characterises his sudden inability to navigate Bristol as 'ludicrous', but 'more of a nuisance than anything'. Apparently it's probably a side effect of the medication. It makes her laugh a bit at first, because he's always been terrible with directions, but not that terrible.

EVA:

The young woman's insides are quietly jangling like jars in a cupboard at the first shake of an earthquake.
She calls her dad.

PETE:

"<u>Hullo</u>"

EVA:

He says it with a 'u' in place of the 'e'. He asks about Bella's morning.

7

BELLA:

"Are you alright, Dad? You sound a bit... manic or something."

EVA:

There's a frenetic energy, an intensity bubbling just below the surface of his words that she can't identify.

PETE:

"Do I? I'm sitting in the hospital canteen with Deb. We've just been talking to the neurologist about the results of my follow-up brain scan."

BELLA:

"Oh right."

PETE:

"It turns out it wasn't encephalitis after all."

BELLA:

"Okay."

EVA:

The balloon in the middle of her is swelling.

PETE:

"The scans show that what they thought was the virus has grown, in a way that only a tumour does. They're going to do a biopsy, but he's pretty certain that I have a brain tumour. The reason they mistook it for encephalitis is that it's very diffuse, which means it would be impossible to operate on."

BELLA:

"What does that mean?"

PETE:

"Well, I asked him if, short of me getting run over by a bus tomorrow, this was going to kill me, and he said yes."

EVA:

The air has flown out of her.

BELLA:

"I'm so sorry, Dad. I'm so sorry."

PETE:

"<u>I'M sorry.</u>"

EVA:

*Tears pour out of her eyes, snot pours down her face. She wipes it off
with her hands, and wipes her hands on the grass.*

BELLA:

"I don't know what to say."

PETE:

"<u>No, neither do I</u>."

EVA:

Her heart punches out of her chest, desperately grasping for her dad.

BELLA:

"Do you have any idea how long?"

PETE:

"<u>No. Well, they're letting me go home and are scheduling
the biopsy for a couple of days' time, so I guess probably not
today, but no</u>."

***

<u>A LOGICAL, PHILOSOPHICAL GUIDE TO MANAGING MORTALITY</u>

GUIDE:

Good evening, and welcome to 'A Logical, Philosophical Guide
to Managing Mortality'. I'm Isobel, I'll be taking you through
the 17 Steps to Conquering Death, and this is my assistant, Eva.

ASSISTANT:
Hello!

GUIDE:
You just saw a re-enactment depicting a young woman on the telephone to her father in August of 2010. I will be using this woman as a case study. You saw her find out that her father was going to die. For her, this is something known as an 'out of context problem'.

This is not just a disaster; it is something that radically alters the context in which a person is living. For example, if Earth were invaded by aliens.

(ASSISTANT plays silly spooky alien music on the piano.)

For the subject of our case study, it is not just very sad that her father is dying; to her, nothing makes sense anymore. This is obviously ridiculous. Death is entirely to be expected.

(ASSISTANT plays Jaws' theme on piano, interrupting the following.)

Everyone you love is going to die. In fact, everyone you meet is going to die.

(GUIDE stops ASSISTANT and she gets up from the piano to demonstrate the following.)

With that in mind, we are going to start with a simple exercise. Eva and I will demonstrate. First, I'd like you to turn to your neighbour and introduce yourself, thus:

GUIDE:
"Hello, I'm Isobel."

ASSISTANT:
"Hello, I'm Eva."

GUIDE:
Next, you will tell your neighbour that they are going to die, like so:

GUIDE:
"You are going to die."

(ASSISTANT becomes incredibly distressed and afraid, and GUIDE has to calm her down and remind her that it is just an exercise before she can continue.)

ASSISTANT:

"You are going to die."

GUIDE:
Finally, you will shake hands. Okay, your turn. *(Waits for audience to comply.)* Good.

When you do experience the death of a loved one, you should <u>avoid reacting to their perfectly normal mortality as if it were as unexpected as an alien invasion</u>.

(ASSISTANT plays silly spooky alien music on the piano again. GUIDE cuts her off.)

You should approach it in a logical manner. That is why we're here; to learn the secret to effectively managing mortality. All you need are the <u>17 Steps to Conquering Death</u>.

STEP 1: ACCEPT THE NEWS

Namely, someone you love is going to die, probably quite soon.

(ASSISTANT shakes head and smiles, reassuring the audience that no one is really going to die.)

Upon receiving the bad news, many people enter a state of <u>denial</u>. This <u>is</u> clearly <u>pointless</u>. It won't change anything, and it will waste time, so don't do it. <u>Accept it immediately</u>.

***

SCENE 2
(Tube train, afternoon.)

EVA:

Bella is melting. Her muscle is shrinking. Pfffft. She sits, a deflated balloon, leaking tears indiscriminately. The commuters sitting opposite her, fleshed out and upright, breathing as though it were easy, are a million miles away and further every moment.

BELLA:

"My dad is going to die my dad is going to die my dad is going to die my dad is going to die."

***

GUIDE:

<u>Acceptance will be distressing</u>. If you think you're fine, you're in denial. If you're a blubbering mess, you're on the right track.

STEP 2: GO AND BE WITH YOUR DYING LOVED ONE

Your loved one lives in Bristol. <u>Get the train to Bristol immediately</u>.

STEP-OUT 1

WRITER:

Hi. So, when I was seven I moved with my mum from Bristol to York. So every school holiday for eleven years I had a five-hour train journey down to Bristol to visit my dad, Pete.

At the end of the visits, he would get the train back with me. Five hours on the train, ten minutes in York station, and five hours back. When Maisie (my half sister) got a bit older, she'd come along too. At the station, we'd all pile into the photo booth and take silly pictures, and Pete would cut the strip in half and I'd take two and they'd take two.

When he hugged me goodbye he would squeeze me so tight it would squash my face. It made me feel guilty for telling the court officer I wanted to live with my mum. I'd wonder if he knew.

GUIDE:
Once in the correct city, accompany your loved one to hospital. They will require a brain biopsy in order to diagnose the type of brain tumour they have. This is an intricate surgical procedure. At present, it is provided free of charge by the National Health Service.

ASSISTANT:
Ladies and gentlemen, please join in with the NHS anthem!

(Plays piano to tune of 'God Save the Queen.')

GUIDE:
(Stands reverentially and sings; loud, confident, out of tune. Gestures for the audience to join in.)

Please save our N H S
Long live our N H S
Our N H S
Welfare victorious
Healthy and glorious
Long to protect us
Save N H S

When your loved one is in need of brain surgery, you will find that the NHS is considerably more helpful than the queen, so please remember those words.

ASSISTANT:
I used to get all my clothes at NHS.

GUIDE:
That's not–

The biopsy is an <u>inpatient procedure</u>, so your loved one will stay in hospital overnight. Remain with them for as long as possible and return first thing in the morning to take them home.

STEP 3: HUGS

(ASSISTANT runs over and hugs GUIDE. GUIDE tries to ignore her holding her. ASSISTANT does increasingly silly holds, with legs etc.)

GUIDE:
You will feel a strong desire for emotional intimacy with your loved one. This is best achieved through the physical proximity provided by a hug.
<u>Numerous studies have shown hugs to provide scientifically observable health benefits, such as boosting oxytocin and serotonin levels</u>.

However, <u>you must hug properly in order to achieve these positive effects</u>.

Let's practice now. Everybody stand up. Eva and I will demonstrate the correct grip.

(GUIDE and ASSISTANT demonstrate throughout the following. ASSISTANT gets it wrong at first.)

Place your <u>right arm over the shoulder</u>, and your <u>left arm under the armpit</u>, around the ribcage. Pull in and <u>press your chests together</u>, placing your <u>head over the right shoulder</u>.

<u>Turn to your neighbour now and follow these steps</u>.

In order to release the relevant hormones, it is necessary to hold this position for a <u>minimum of ten seconds</u>.

(GUIDE waits for audience to comply, then removes glasses, as if for ease in demonstrating the hug. Pause. ASSISTANT slips out of hug, returns to piano.)

***

SCENE 3
(Front hall, early evening.)
(BELLA hugging (empty space as) Pete. Piano. Hold.)

***

STEP 4: ASK QUESTIONS

(Throughout the following, ASSISTANT is raising her hand and trying to get GUIDE's attention, to ask a question: 'Is it time for my song?')

GUIDE:
You will have lots of questions. Ask all of them. <u>Don't be embarrassed or ashamed of wanting to know what you're dealing with.</u>

You will get the results of the biopsy a week after the operation: <u>Glioblastoma multiforme grade 4.</u>

(ASSISTANT sings an inappropriate but earnest rock ballad using the phrase 'glioblastoma multiforme grade 4'. Holds up APPLAUSE sign at the end.)

GUIDE:
This is the most serious, aggressive, malignant tumour.
<u>It is too diffuse to operate on.</u> There are treatment options; chemotherapy or radiotherapy might buy you some time.

You will need to know how much time, in order to determine whether you should remain in Bristol, or return to London.

First, request a ballpark figure. Ask the doctor if your loved one's life expectancy would be most appropriately measured in years, or days. When the doctor looks at you as if you just punched her in the face, and turns uncertainly to your loved one, and asks if they want to know, explain to the doctor that of course your loved one wants to know. This is the person whose final wish is to read a particularly challenging maths textbook! Your loved one does not require talking down to. When the Occupational Therapist was checking your loved one's brain functions after the biopsy, they answered the maths questions before she had time to start the stopwatch. Your loved one loves numbers.

ASSISTANT:
Give him some fucking numbers!

GUIDE:
That doctor won't give you any numbers. But the oncologist will. Being a cancer specialist, she will be more accustomed to talking to dying people, and so she will estimate how long your loved one has left to live; approximately two months. With treatment, maybe two more.

ASSISTANT:
Yay!

GUIDE:
You will choose a short, intense course of radiotherapy.

STEP 5: FEEL HELPLESS

You will do this for two reasons:

1) It is a key step towards accepting the reality of mortality.
2) It is unavoidable.

One morning, your loved one will wake up with a headache. You will know it's bad, because when you go into the bedroom, they won't even try to smile at you. They will be blinded by the pain, eyes dull and swimming. Someone will call an ambulance. Your loved one will be heavy, unsteady, groping. They won't cry out, they'll just cloud over. And vomit.

***

SCENE 4
(Hospital, morning.)

BELLA:

"Somebody help him. Please, help him.
Help him. Help him. Help him."

***

STEP 6: BE HELPFUL

GUIDE:
As your loved one's health deteriorates, they will lose the ability to perform even the most basic bodily functions without assistance. This will give you the opportunity to be helpful. They will require <u>personal care</u>. This is the term used to refer to <u>assisting an ill or disabled person with washing, dressing and toileting</u>.

If your loved–one is male, you will need to familiarise yourself with –

ASSISTANT:
(Presenting prop.)
The portable urinal!

GUIDE:
It is designed to lie flat on the bed, with the tip of the penis at the opening –

ASSISTANT
(Panicking, to GUIDE.)
I don't have a penis!

GUIDE:
No, that's perfectly natural.

(ASSISTANT asks various audience members if she can borrow their penis, including women; 'You don't have one either? How does that make you feel?' etc.)

GUIDE:
Stop asking to borrow a penis!

(ASSISTANT has an idea: gets GUIDE's pink water bottle from side of stage and holds it as if it were her penis. GUIDE hesitates, then continues.)

GUIDE:
The portable urinal is designed to lie flat on the bed, with the tip of the penis at the opening so that the urine flows down here.

(ASSISTANT pours water from the bottle-as-penis into urinal to demonstrate.)

If your loved one is lying on his back in bed, you may find that he struggles to reach the opening with his penis. You will then be tempted to tip the urinal towards him to make it easier.

(ASSISTANT tips urinal, inadvertently pouring water onto sheet.)

<u>Do not tip the urinal</u>. It is angled down for a reason. If you tip it, the urine will flow straight back out, and onto the sheet.

In the likely eventuality that you fail to heed this advice, you will need to change the sheet. I will now demonstrate how to do this, with your incapacitated loved one in the bed.

Eva will play the part of your loved one.

(ASSISTANT tries to get a volunteer from the audience: 'A lovely volunteer!' etc. GUIDE refuses: 'Eva will play the part of your loved one. Sir/madam, sit down.' etc. ASSISTANT returns to the bed.)

ASSISTANT:
(To GUIDE.)
It's wet.

GUIDE:
Yes, that's because you tipped the urinal.

(ASSISTANT reluctantly lies on top of the stain. Whilst speaking, GUIDE does the actions specified throughout the following.)

First <u>place a clean sheet</u> along the edge of the bed opposite you. Then bend your loved one's knees up, and <u>roll them towards you</u>.

(GUIDE crouches down so that her head is level with ASSISTANT, who turns to look at her. Puts glasses on her head to make eye contact and–)

***

SCENE 5
(Living room, afternoon.)

BELLA

You alright there, Dad? Sorry about this. I'll be done
in a minute.

***

(GUIDE replaces glasses and continues demonstration.)

GUIDE:
Next, <u>roll up the soiled sheet</u> and push it under your loved one's side. It is at this juncture that you should <u>clean the buttocks</u>.

ASSISTANT:
Yes!

GUIDE:
Baby wipes are usually sufficient.

When that is done, <u>spread the clean sheet</u> over the exposed half of the bed and tuck the excess under their side as well. This will of course be easier on your loved one's bed, as it will be much wider. *(Awkwardly attempting a joke.)* Or at least I hope so; don't make your loved one sleep on a bench!

Next, <u>roll your loved one onto their back</u>. <u>Walk around</u> to the other side, then <u>roll them towards you</u> again. You can now <u>pull out the dirty sheet</u> –

ASSISTANT:
Tada!

GUIDE:
– and <u>spread the clean sheet</u> over this half of the bed. Make sure you smooth it; <u>wrinkles</u> are uncomfortable, and <u>can cause bedsores</u> with immobile individuals.

Roll your loved one back to their original position, and the process is complete.

(ASSISTANT silently insists on GUIDE getting the APPLAUSE sign. Then gets up, bows proudly etc.)

STEP 7: ADOPT A MOTTO

GUIDE:
As death draws closer, the perspective from which you view the world will shift dramatically. Things that previously seemed important, like whether you had showered before leaving the house, will lose all significance. Things that you barely noticed before, like the creases in the skin on your loved ones hands, will become momentous. <u>A motto will help you adjust to the new context in which you are living</u>. The best motto is:

GUIDE & ASSISTANT:
'<u>These are the days of miracle and wonder.</u>'

STEP-OUT 2

WRITER:

That's not a common motto; it's a line from a Paul Simon song – 'The Boy In The Bubble'. Deb (my dad's girlfriend of over 20 years) told us about it. My sister Maisie and I didn't know the song, but we latched onto this line instantly. Pete was being amazing; he said he felt very lucky, he'd had a great time, and he just felt a bit embarrassed to be leaving the party early. We were trying to follow his lead. This line summed it up somehow – these are the days of miracle and wonder. These days, even as your dad is dying, and your heart is actually literally aching (like in the songs). These are the days. Right now. They are all you've got.

GUIDE:
You may feel that because someone you love is dying, everything is terrible. You are wrong. <u>The world is just as it was</u>.

ASSISTANT:
Yay!

GUIDE:
When your loved one was healthy, and you were carefree, someone else's loved one was dying of a brain tumour.

ASSISTANT:
Yay!

GUIDE:
<u>Your personal crisis has not obliterated all good from the surface of the planet</u>.

ASSISTANT:
Yay!

***

SCENE 6

(Living Room. Afternoon.)
*(Throughout the following, BELLA strings up white paper chains
and puts on a fascinator.)*

EVA:
Pete and Deb are getting married.

STEP-OUT 3

WRITER:

They didn't believe in marriage, but a friend told them this
would make the paperwork easier when Pete died. Deb
broke it to Pete as bad news. But Maisie and I decided if they
were gonna get married, we were gonna have a wedding
goddammit. And be bridesmaids.

EVA:

*The sofas fill with family and friends and flowers and cake.
Pete's hand shakes as he signs the register. Deb looks at him, her
damp eyes shining, reaching out from her tired face. She looks
beautiful.*

Music dances between bubbling voices. Bella feels at home.

WRITER:

Pete's mum and dad would have been married fifty years
the following day.

There was going to be a big family party in the country.
They cancelled it.

***

STEP 8: ADAPT

GUIDE:
Death doesn't cooperate. It will deviate from your carefully planned treatment schedule. <u>Adaptability is a key skill.</u> <u>Develop it</u>.

Your loved one will have an appointment at the hospital a few days before they are due to start radiotherapy, to verify that they are ready.

You will meet with the consultant oncologist. It will be <u>the fastest growing tumour she has ever seen</u>.

ASSISTANT:
Ooo-ooh!

GUIDE:
She will explain that <u>given the size of the tumour, treatment is unlikely to work</u>. If it did extend your loved one's life, it would hold them in a state of very poor health, in which they may not want to be held. You will decide not to go ahead with treatment.

***

SCENE 7
(Hospital, afternoon.)
(BELLA sits, cradling PETE's head.)

EVA:

Pete looks at Bella as if through a fog. He is like a baby bird, and beside him, Bella is solid. Shaky, but substantial.

The doctor's features are struggling to stay where they're supposed to be. Shock contorts the lines of her face. The doctor's eyes are wet. The doctor is sorry.

Now Bella is very small and very scared.

***

STEP 9: RESIST THE FALSE ALLURE OF A DEITY

GUIDE:

Your loved one will stop eating. Their cheeks will become sunken. Before long, they will struggle even to drink, and you will moisten their dry mouth with a pink medical sponge on the end of a small white plastic stick,

(ASSISTANT presents prop medical sponge to demonstrate.)

which you will dip in water and gently wipe around their gums.

You will realise that they are actually going to die.

However, it will be impossible to imagine the person ceasing to exist. You may be tempted to imagine instead that –

ASSISTANT:
(Happily.)
Your loved one will go to heaven!

GUIDE:
(Surpised.)
It is comforting to think that –

ASSISTANT:
(With absoluie conviction.)
There is an all-powerful god who loves us!

GUIDE:
(Irritated.)
And that that god will ensure that –

ASSISTANT:
(Reassuring.)
The death of their body will not be the end of the person you love.

GUIDE:
(Angry.)

However, <u>there is no heaven</u>. And <u>there is no god</u>. *(To ASSISTANT, gesturing to piano stool.)* Sit down.

(ASSISTANT sits on the floor and cries.)

Your loved one is suffering horribly as an inoperable tumour eats away at their brain. An all-powerful, all-loving god could prevent their suffering, so <u>why is there suffering</u>? If there is a god, then that god is responsible for the evil that is your loved one's suffering. That god does not love you.

ASSISTANT:
(Jumping to her feet, pronouncing it incorrectly.)
The Irenaean Theodicy!

GUIDE:
(With correct pronunciation.)
The <u>Irenaean Theodicy</u> –

ASSISTANT:
That's what I said.

GUIDE:
– claims that we are wrong to assume that an all-loving god wouldn't want us to suffer. In fact, Irenaeus argues, <u>god does want us to suffer, because</u> –

ASSISTANT:
<u>It's good for us</u>.

GUIDE:
He explains that humans are imperfect, and <u>a world with suffering gives us the opportunity to develop good moral qualities</u>.

ASSISTANT:
Suffering makes us better people.

GUIDE:
That's plausible. Then the pertinent question becomes *(to ASSISTANT)*: <u>How much suffering is enough?</u>

(ASSISTANT makes a confident gesture with her hands to show an amount (of suffering). GUIDE looks unconvinced. ASSISTANT, unsure, moves hands to a different amount, then another, then gives up and returns to piano, cowed.)

Let us return to our case study. Let's say that when our subject was four years old, her mother was diagnosed with a neurological condition, called multiple sclerosis. What if, due to this condition, the mother gradually loses the ability to walk, and loses control of her bowels, and lies awake at night afraid that she won't be able to care for her daughter, but smiles through the day and encourages the daughter and hugs her and plays word games at the dinner table? *(Lowering glasses part way.)* Will that be enough Irenaeus?

No? What if her arms seize up and her hands become claws, so the daughter has to put flannels under her fingers to stop her nails cutting her palms, and she can't feed herself, or wash herself, or change the channel on the TV, and good-hearted people do all of those things for her, and she keeps smiling and saying thank you? *(Lowering glasses part way.)* Is that enough?

What if her throat becomes so weak that she can't swallow, so she has to have a tube go directly into her stomach to feed her, and she can never taste chocolate again, and she can't vocalise enough sound to speak properly, so she can never fully express herself, and still she smiles, and mouths 'I love you' every time she sees her daughter? *(Removing glasses.)* Is her soul good enough yet, Irenaeus?

No matter how many clever arguments we come up with to try and convince ourselves otherwise, <u>life is not fair</u>. Mean, lazy people win the lottery, and kind, generous people get cancer. <u>Nature is impartial, indifferent, random</u>. This is terrifying. But it is true.

Sometimes, terrible things happen and it's nobody's fault. And if you're filled with fury at your powerlessness to save someone you love, you just have to yell at the sky. And then go back inside and quietly hold that someone's hand, and hope it helps. *(She walks to side of stage and has some water, does not act in the following scene.)*

***

SCENE 8
(Pete's living room, afternoon.)

EVA:

The afternoon glows softly through the window. Pete's breath ebbs and flows, lapping the bedclothes.

Bella nestles down and takes shelter beneath her dad's earlobe. He is warm. His chin is bristly, and his cheek is soft. She looks up, and sees one rogue eyebrow strand curling eccentrically up towards his hairline, and hooking into a furrow on his forehead. She feels his heart beat resonate through her, steady and even.

***

STEP 10: SAY ANYTHING THAT YOU WILL REGRET NOT HAVING SAID

GUIDE:
Say it now. This is your last chance.

***

SCENE 9
(Living room, evening.)
(BELLA sits on the sofa, looking at PETE.)

EVA:

Bella has a sort of queasiness in the pit of her stomach. She wants to hold her dad as tightly as he held her every time she left him at York station. And she never wants to let go.

BELLA:

"Dad, I'm so sorry I wasn't here more, when I was younger."

PETE:

"<u>Don't be silly; it wasn't your fault</u>."

***

<u>STEP 11: TELL PEOPLE YOU VOLE THEM</u>

***

SCENE 10

(Living room, evening.)
(BELLA sitting on the sofa.)

EVA:

Bella floats in the indigo sky, reflected in the dark panes of the window. Pete is sleeping. His friend Andrew is reading. Pete coughs awake, abruptly.

BELLA:

"Hey Dad, you alright?"

<u>ANDREW:</u>

"<u>What you thinkin?</u>"

BELLA:

"Do you want a drink?"

BELLA:

"Are you in pain?"

<u>PETE:</u>

"<u>No</u>."

BELLA:

"Good. I love you. Sorry, we're asking a lot of questions, aren't we? We ought to be entertaining you. I'm not very good at witty repartee. I keep trying to think of different ways of saying 'I love you', so I don't get boring."

PETE:

"Tricky, isn't it?"

ANDREW:

"How about anagrams?"

PETE:

"That's definitely the best approach."

BELLA:

"Okay, so can I say 'I vole you'? Or do I have to mix up all the words?"

ANDREW:

"That is what you must say."

BELLA:

"Okay. I vole you."

***

STEP 12: HOWL

***

SCENE 11
(BELLA's temporary bedroom. Morning.)

EVA:

Stripes of morning light filter through the blinds. Bella is woken by a knock at the door.

BELLA:

"Come in."

EVA:

DEB stands in the doorway, sleepy-faced.

DEB:

"<u>He's gone</u>."

BELLA/WRITER:

My dad is dead. I hug him, kiss him, hold him. Feel his weight and his warmth and his smell one last time, before it's all gone.

I love you, Dad. I love you.

But my love just balls up in a knot in my chest; it doesn't escape as words, because you're not there to hear my words.

As a concept, death was slippery and mysterious; unimaginable; impossible. But as a physical fact, it's brutally simple. You're gone. I force myself to look at you. Your skin's already turning waxy. Your eyes are empty. I keep looking, until I know it's true; your body's here, but it's like a photo: you're not in it.

The district nurse comes, and she helps Deb and I wash you. When we turn you on your side, the blood in your veins makes groovy, spacey patterns in your back. Deep purple flowers, splotchily, up against translucent skin, and then eases towards the mattress; there's no pumping heart to fight gravity now.

"Wow," Deb exclaims, "I wish you could see this, you'd love it." And you would.

We slide your stiffening limbs into the robot t-shirt Maisie made you, and your favourite shorts, and some thick, comfy socks. Andrew gently shaves the stubble from your dead face. And you look so beautiful. You look like the dad I love.

There are a number of little treasures you kept in your wallet – photos, and little drawings and notes. Deb takes them out, makes copies of them, and then slips the originals into your pockets, for you to take with you. Among these things that you have carried everywhere with you, for years, is a scrap of paper, with a shopping list jotted down in your familiar handwriting, and in the corner, the larger, rounder letters of a child spell out: 'I love my dad. Bella', and two kisses, with a circle drawn round them.

EVA:

Bella's torso is slowly collapsing in on itself, crushing her insides, and she doesn't have to be strong for her dad anymore, so she walks calmly downstairs and outside into the small back garden.

(BELLA kneels down on all fours and howls three times. Then she stands.)

The undertakers came. Real undertakers, like off the telly, and they zipped Pete into a body bag, and wheeled him out on a stretcher. As they descended the front steps, a group of teenage boys rounded the corner, joking and chatting. One of the boys glanced over, saw us, and hushed his friends. I suddenly saw the scene through his eyes; a family, standing teary-eyed in their doorway, as a loved one is carried away. One of those terribly sad things that happen to other people.

That evening, we left the house. We walked across Brandon Hill. It was October now, and the air was clear and cool. The city stretched out into the dark, glimmering squares of light. The sky was… vast.

(Piano. Stillness.)

***

STEP 13: PLAN THE FUNERAL

GUIDE:
A funeral is a wonderful opportunity to <u>celebrate the life of your loved one</u>.

Bury your loved one in a <u>memorial woodland</u>, so that as their body decays, they feed the trees, and become part of nature.

Choose an attractive <u>wicker casket</u>, and weave fresh flowers into it. This will be a way of expressing your love one last time.

Select a <u>humanist celebrant</u> to lead the ceremony. The service will be beautiful. Hundreds of people will come, and you will feel proud of your loved one.

Try to find comfort in an allegorical tale that has at its core the <u>first law of thermodynamics</u>, which states that <u>no energy is created in the universe, and none is destroyed</u>.

***

SCENE 12
(Memorial woodlands chapel, afternoon.)

BELLA:

Hello. Wow, there are so many of you. Thank you for coming. I'd like to share with you a little story from a book called 'Tuesdays with Morrie', by Mitch Albom.

Okay. The story is about a little wave, bobbing along in the ocean, having a grand old time. He's enjoying the wind and the fresh air – until he notices the other waves in front of him, crashing against the shore.

'My God, this is terrible,'

the wave says.

'Look what's going to happen to me!'

Then along comes another wave. It sees the first wave, looking grim, and it says to him,

'Why do you look so sad?'

The first wave says,

'You don't understand! We're all going to crash! All of us waves are going to be nothing! Isn't it terrible?'

The second wave says,

'No, you don't understand. You're not a wave, you're part of the ocean.'

STEP 14: TRY TO BE HAPPY

GUIDE:

<u>Your loved one is dead,</u> and <u>there is nothing you can do to bring them back.</u> Being sad won't bring them back. Your loved one wouldn't want you to be sad.

<u>Your loved one would want you to be happy</u>!

(GUIDE and ASSISTANT suddenly dance madly to a section of 'Happy' by Pharrell Williams, then regain complete control for–)

GUIDE:

A month of mourning after the funeral will be sufficient. Remember

GUIDE & ASSISTANT:
<u>You are not dead!</u>
<u>You did not die!</u>

STEP 15: REMEMBER YOUR LOVED ONE

GUIDE:

You carry part of their identity in your mind. You must keep them alive.

Read the comics they liked. Listen to the music on their iPod. Complete the puzzle they started.

STEP 16: GET OUT OF BED

GUIDE:

After a few months of trying to be happy and remembering your loved one, you will feel like you have done enough. You have been strong.

ASSISTANT:
You did it!

GUIDE:
You deserve a break. You deserve to wake up one morning, and find that just for a day –

ASSISTANT:
Your loved one is back, and everything's fine!

GUIDE:
But that's not how science works.

ASSISTANT:
(Losing her temper, mocks GUIDE's previous line, then bursts out with–)

You said this was going to be a MUSICAL!!

GUIDE:
Every morning, you will wake up, and your loved one will still be dead. You still have to get up. However...

STEP 17: FEEL BETTER

GUIDE:
After a couple of years of getting out of bed every day,

GUIDE & ASSITANT:
You will feel better!

GUIDE:
You will start to care about shallow insignificant things again, like whether your clothes match. You will remember to ask other people questions about themselves and actually listen to the answers. You will meet new people, and say in passing 'My dad died a couple of years ago.' And it will sound almost normal.

GUIDE & ASSITANT:
Congratulations! You have conquered death!

(ASSISTANT, who is now very, very happy, sings and a short celebratory song about conquering death. The lyrics begin to suggest that no one will die anymore. GUIDE attempts to interrupt, to correct her.)

GUIDE:

Of course you have not eradicated death. Death is unavoidable. But you have effectively managed your response to it. You have not allowed death to destroy you. You should be proud of yourself. Give yourselves a round of applause.

(GUIDE shakes people's hands, congratulating them 'Well done. You're doing very well. That's the tricky bit over and done with now. It's plain sailing from here. You've mastered the steps haven't you? Yes, so there's no need to be upset any more.' etc. It feels like a short break in proceedings. After a time, EVA starts to speak the text below, and GUIDE turns to listen, then slowly walks back to the edge of the stage, and stands with her back to the audience, watching the scene on the screen.)

***

SCENE 13
(Tube platform, evening.)

EVA:

The Tube platform is bustling with rush hour bodies. Bella is pulled up, taught, beneath the strips of electric yellow.

Bella's mother has been admitted to hospital with pneumonia.

DOCTOR:

<u>Your mother's temperature is dangerously low. We are using a warming blanket to keep it stable, but there is a chance it may drop further, and if it doesn't increase soon, she may not recover</u>.

BELLA:

<u>Um, okay, so you're saying there's a risk she won't survive?</u>

DOCTOR:

I'm afraid there is. If the antibiotics take effect, she could make a full recovery, but at the moment, her condition is critical.

BELLA:

Um right, okay, so in terms of timings, how, uh – should I come now? I mean, I'm in London, so it would take me a few hours, but–

DOCTOR:

Yes, I would suggest that you come this evening.

BELLA:

Alright, um I've got to get home and then to the train station – I probably won't arrive until quite late, maybe, I don't know, around ten o' clock. Will that be okay; will they let me onto the ward?

DOCTOR:

Yes, that's fine. I'll let the nursing staff know you're on your way.

BELLA:

Okay, thank you.

***

GUIDE:
(Stepping onto stage, confident, and upbeat.)
Welcome to:

A LOGICAL, PHILOSOPHICAL GUIDE TO MANAGING MORTALITY
PART 2: SUBSEQUENT DEATHS

You just saw the subject from our case study find out that her mother may die. You will have noticed that her response was impressively calm and logical this time. This is because she has a Logical, Philosophical Guide to follow, which makes her mother's mortality eminently more manageable.

In this shorter, second part, we are going to quickly look at how efficiently you will be able to manage subsequent incidents of mortality, once you have experienced your first significant bereavement, and mastered the 17 Steps to Conquering Death. You won't waste any time letting emotions get in the way this time. You have already faced death.

ASSISTANT:
It can't get you again!

GUIDE:
You know that all you have to do, is

GUIDE & ASSISTANT:
follow the guide, step by step!

GUIDE:
You remember the steps, don't you? Say them with me! She says the number, we say the step!

STEP 1: ACCEPT THE NEWS

GUIDE:
Well done! This step will be much easier the second time. This is because <u>death is no longer an out of context problem!</u> You are lucky!

Now that you are familiar with the process, the news that another person you love is going to die will fit perfectly into your worldview. <u>Rather than seeming impossible, the death of your loved one will seem inevitable!</u>

You will accept your loved one's death as a certainty before the doctors have even confirmed the prognosis.

STEP 2: GO AND BE WITH YOUR DYING LOVED ONE

***

SCENE 14
(Yasmin's hospital room, night.)

EVA:

Bella braces herself against the hospital room, her muscles contracting into armour. Under the spotlight of the lamp lies her mother, swallowed up by a cocoon of warming blanket.

She catches sight of Bella, and life rushes around her face like fireflies. Her mouth makes the familiar shape of her daughter's name: 'Bella', she breathes. 'Bella, Bella, Bella...'

BELLA:

"Hello mum."

***

STEP 3: HUGS

(ASSISTANT encourages audience to stand and hug again: 'Hugs! Come on, you remember!' etc. Demonstrates with someone on front row. GUIDE tries to stop her; 'Stop hugging! No hugs this time!' etc.)

The second time you experience the mortality of a loved one, due to your loved one's disability, their upper body mobility will be severely restricted. Their arms will be permanently bent at the elbow, and their hands will be curled in at the wrists. Therefore they will not be capable of partaking in the correct hugging grip.

This brings us to an important principle of the Guide regarding all subsequent incidents of mortality: <u>if for any reason it is not possible to complete a step</u>, don't worry.

This is simply an opportunity to streamline your mortality management. Just move directly onto the next step.

(GUIDE clicks at ASSISTANT to prompt–)

STEP 4: ASK QUESTIONS

GUIDE:
You know how to handle this by now. Information is power.

***

SCENE 15
(Hospital ward, morning.)

BELLA:

Can I speak to you outside for a moment, doctor? Thank you. Can you give me as much information as possible on my mother's condition? I know you can't know anything for certain, and you hate to give numbers in case they turn out to be wrong, but I won't hold you to anything, I'd just like to have a clear understanding of what the possible scenarios are, and the relative likelihood of the various outcomes. And don't worry about tiptoeing around things – I appreciate bluntness.

***

STEP 5: FEEL HELPLESS

About a week later, you will meet with the medical consultant, who will inform you that they are of the opinion that your loved one is dying, and so they will no longer be attempting to treat them with a view to recovery. There is nothing more to be done. Instead, they will hand over to the palliative care team, who specialise in ensuring patients are kept comfortable at the end of their lives.

***

SCENE 16

(Doctor's office, hospital ward, daytime.)
(BELLA sits, facing the consultant and palliative team leader.)

BELLA:

Yes, I understand. Thank you for explaining it to me.

Um, you said you're of the opinion that she's dying. Do you, um, would you be able to estimate how long she has left?

DOCTOR:

I would say probably one to three days.

BELLA:

One to three days. Okay. Thank you.

EVA:

The ballon in Bella–

***

(GUIDE cuts across to announce the next step.)

STEP 6: BE HELPFUL

GUIDE:

The full-time carers who looked after your loved one at home will visit the hospital every day and take responsibility for all personal care, so there won't be anything for you to do. Move on to the next step.

STEP 7: ADOPT A MOTTO

GUIDE:

Keep the same motto, for efficiency's sake. You remember the motto! What was it? Say it with me!

GUIDE & ASSISTANT:
'These are the days of miracle and wonder'!

GUIDE:
Yes! So act in accordance with your motto. Look for the
beauty in the world. Don't just mope around; celebrate!

ASSISTANT:
(Throwing fake snow.)
It's nearly Christmas!

GUIDE:
And your lovely, thoughtful partner has come to keep you
company in the hospital, and they have bought Christmas
decorations and ready-spiced mulled wine and mince pies to
cheer you up. So be grateful and get into the festive spirit.

ASSISTANT:
(Offering GUIDE a mince pie.)
Have a mince pie!

GUIDE:
(Confused.)
No thanks.

ASSISTANT:
You love mince pies! Go on!

GUIDE:
(Taking the pie.)
Sorry – where did you get this? I mean; it's June. *(Say correct
month. Cut line for performances around Christmas.)*

ASSISTANT:
Eat it.

GUIDE:
What's in it?

ASSISTANT:
Eat it.

GUIDE:
But –

ASSISTANT:
(Going back to piano.)
Eat it.

(Both remove glasses. BELLA takes a bite of the mince pie.)

***

SCENE 17
(Hospital room, evening.)
(BELLA hangs Christmas decorations around the room.)

BELLA:

This is nice, isn't mum? Bit of festive cheer, brighten the room
up a bit? Do you like these gold baubles? Can you see them
there? Yeah?

(Piano begins to play 'Silent Night.' BELLA looks out to the corridor.)

BELLA:

Oh wow. There are carol singers out in the ward. Mum, can
you hear them?

(BELLA goes and sits with Yasmin during the following.)

ASSISTANT as CAROL SINGERS:
(Sings.)

Silent night, Holy night
All is calm, all is bright
Round yon virgin, mother and child
Holy infant, tender and mild
Sleep in heavenly peace,
Sleep in heavenly peace.

(Piano & singing end. Silence. Stillness.)

***

STEP 8: ADAPT

GUIDE:

As you know, death does not co-operate. Three days will go by. Then four, then five, then six. And still your loved one will not die, irrespective of the consultant's prognosis. You will have to cancel the birthday party you planned months ago, and wait. And just hope your loved one doesn't die on your actual birthday.

STEP 9: RESIST THE FALSE ALLURE OF A DEITY

GUIDE:

There still isn't a god. That much should be glaringly obvious by now.

(GUIDE looks to ASSISTANT, daring her to contradict this. ASSISTANT looks down, and plays the intro for–)

STEP 10: SAY ANYTHING THAT YOU WILL REGRET NOT HAVING SAID

***

SCENE 18

BELLA:

How could you rob me of a father? Were you so insecure and neurotic that all you could do was run away? Run away to York – where we had no friends, where I had no dad. What the fuck was your problem?

Oh, I know you were afraid you'd be sidelined as the MS got worse – the disabled black single mother versus the healthy white man with a new happy family – the knight on a white horse swooping in and stealing me from you.

Did it ever occur to you that not everything is about you and your shit? That I might want the knight on a horse? Or that the knight was an actual person who loved me?

Why should I feel guilty for not fighting you on it? You should have known better. You were the grown-up.

And now he's gone, and I'll never see him again, and now you're going to die too, and I'll have no one.

***

STEP-OUT 4

WRITER:

I didn't say that to my mum. I kept my emotions completely under control at all times. Saying it now makes me feel like a traitor. It's kind of thrilling, throwing it out, but it's also a bit like plunging headfirst into a black pit where nothing is good anymore.

<u>STEP 11: TELL PEOPLE YOU VOLE THEM</u>

***

SCENE 19
(Hospital room, evening.)
(BELLA sits at Yasmin's bedside.)

EVA:

Bella looks at her mum, her wide, trusting eyes shining out of her face, child-like in its bloated plumpness. She looks cute; like a baby on the brink of life. And Bella wants to cradle her in her arms, and swaddle her in only good, kind things.

BELLA:

Love you.

***

STEP 12: HOWL

***

SCENE 20
(Hospital room, night.)

EVA:

The sun has set on Bella's birthday.

Bella has pushed the reclining chair as close to her mum's bed as she can, and now she is sleeping on her mum's shoulder, curling into the warmth of her neck, like she did as a baby.

Matt's voice gently nudges her awake.

MATT:

Babe, I think she's gone.

EVA:

Bella looks at her mum. She is still warm, and her eyes are still closed, but her face has set, like stone.

(BELLA looks at Yasmin's face, then nods at Matt.)

EVA:

Matt gets the nurse.

Yes, the nurse says, she's gone. I'm sorry.

(BELLA takes down all the decorations and packs them away. This takes some time. She doesn't cry.)

***

STEP 13: PLAN THE FUNERAL

GUIDE:
As next of kin, you will have a few extra responsibilities to take care of before arranging the funeral, so you will need to remain focused.

1. <u>Inform anyone who knew your loved one of their death</u>.
2. <u>Collect the death certificate from the hospital</u>.
3. <u>Register the death at the local Register Office</u>.

Your loved one will have specified in their will that they wish to be cremated, and have their ashes scattered in the Caribbean. Crematoriums are not very nice places, so do not have the ceremony there. Fortunately, only fifteen people will be attending the funeral, so simplify things by having the service in your loved one's living room.

Select a white cardboard coffin; the sensible choice, as it is the cheapest, and it will be burned the next day anyway.

STEP 14: TRY TO BE HAPPY

GUIDE:
There will be no need to mourn for a whole month the second time around. You'll pretty much bounce right back. Less than a fortnight after the funeral, your partner of nearly nine years will–

GUIDE & ASSISTANT:
(Releasing a solitary party popper.)
Propose!

GUIDE:
With a

GUIDE & ASSISTANT:
sparkling ring

GUIDE:
at the end of a

GUIDE & ASSISTANT:
perfectly planned day

GUIDE:
with a

GUIDE & ASSISTANT:
beautiful speech

GUIDE:
detailing how much you mean to him. Less than a fortnight
after that, you will have a belated

GUIDE & ASSISTANT:
birthday party!

GUIDE:
Because

GUIDE & ASSISTANT:
you deserve some joy

GUIDE:
after everything you've been through. And you'll be surrounded
by

GUIDE & ASSISTANT:
wonderful friends who love you.

GUIDE:
And as they arrive, they'll all say the same three things –

***

SCENE 21

(BELLA's living room, evening.)

*(BELLA makes appropriate expressions in response to the following,
repeating 'thank you' smile, 'that's life' head tilt, and 'yay!' smile
on a loop.)*

ASSISTANT as FRIEND:

Happy birthday! I'm so sorry about your mum. But you're
engaged, congratulations!
Happy birthday! I'm sorry about your mum. You're engaged
though, yay!

Happy birthday darling! Are you okay, I'm so sorry.
And congratulations on your engagement!

Happy birthday to you! Oh, love – I'm so sorry about your
mum. But tonight it's party time, engaged lady!

**

STEP 15: REMEMBER YOUR LOVED ONE

GUIDE:

Don't have so much fun living your life that you forget about
your loved one.

Keep them alive in your thoughts. Remember how they drove
through Paris like a lunatic. Remember how, one half term,
while you were away at your dad's, they bought a puppy,
even though you were both scared of dogs. Remember how
when they were in the hospital, every time you asked them
for a smile, no matter how weak they were, they would give
you the warmest smile in the world.

STEP-OUT 5

WRITER:

When I was younger, I had a recurring nightmare. I'd
forgotten about it, until it came back, after my mum died.

In the dream, I suddenly remember that I was supposed to be
looking after my mum, and I've forgotten about her, and left
her all day. She's been lying in bed; helpless, covered in her
own filth, in pain, hungry, alone and afraid. She's been calling
and calling for someone to help her.

I run up to her room, and I feel sick, because I don't even
have an excuse, I just forgot about her. And I walk in, my
heart in the pit of my stomach, and her sheets are wet, and
her face is crumpled up, and then she sees me, and her eyes

light up, and she's so happy that I'm there. She says my name
over and over, and she's not even cross. She's just so grateful
that I came.

I woke up from the dream still feeling panicked that I was
supposed to be looking after mum, and I'd forgotten. Then I
realised with relief that it wasn't real. And unlike other times
I'd had the dream, I could be absolutely certain it wasn't real,
because she was dead.

STEP 16: GET OUT OF BED

GUIDE:
It's easier to get out of bed when you've got a full day ahead
of you. At first, you will do a fantastic job of keeping busy.
You'll even –

ASSISTANT:
(Throwing more fake snow.)
Go on your first skiing holiday!

GUIDE:
But after a few months, there will come a day when you don't
have any particular reason to get up. It will be past midday,
and you will have had more than enough sleep, but you will
just lie in bed.

***

SCENE 22
(BELLA's bedroom, early afternoon.)
(BELLA is lying in bed, awake.)

EVA:

*Bella wakes up to a feeling of dread. Nausea knots her stomach.
A dull weight presses her down. She is afraid.*

49

GUIDE:

There is nothing to be afraid of. There isn't a monster waiting for you in the living room, is there? Just get out of bed.

EVA:

Bella can't find the strength to face the day.

GUIDE:

That's an incredibly unhelpful metaphor. The day isn't a thing to be faced. You're making the simple act of living sound intimidating.

EVA:

It is intimidating.

GUIDE:

Oh for goodness sake, don't be so pathetic!

BELLA:

My mum is DEAD!

GUIDE:

So? Your mum is going to be dead every day from now on. You're not going to never get out of bed again, are you? Just get up.

BELLA:

I don't want to.

GUIDE:

Great.

BELLA:

I want my mum. And my dad. I want my dad. I want them back. Please. Please come back.

GUIDE:

Who are you talking to? Because you don't believe in god, and your mum and dad don't exist anymore.

BELLA:

Fuck you.

I feel like I'm disappearing.

GUIDE:

Oh good, I see you've lost touch with reality altogether.

BELLA:

This is my reality.

GUIDE:

You're not making any sense.

BELLA:

I know! Nothing makes any sense! Death doesn't make any
sense!

GUIDE:

Okay, indulging in some pathetic image of yourself as a poor
little orphan isn't getting us anywhere.

BELLA:

I am an orphan!

GUIDE:

Yes, a twenty-eight-year-old orphan. It's not like you're off
to the poor house now to live on gruel. You've got a nice life
with a lovely home, a wonderful fiancé, and lots of brilliant
friends. The only real difference being 'an orphan' is going
to make to your day-to-day life is that you won't need to feel
guilty for never calling your mum anymore.

BELLA:

(Guttural wordless yowl of pain.)

GUIDE:

No one said this was going to be easy.

BELLA:

I'm tired. I'm so tired.

GUIDE:

I know. Life is tiring sometimes. You just have to stay strong.

BELLA:

Why? Why do I always have to be strong? I'm tired of being strong.

GUIDE:

Because you don't have any choice. You can't just collapse.

BELLA:

Why not? Why do I always have to look after everyone? Why can't someone look after me for once? Why can I never be weak?

GUIDE:

Who would want to be weak? Weakness is a flaw.

BELLA:

Yes! Humans have flaws. I am a human, and I have flaws. I'm sorry I'm not a perfect logic machine!

GUIDE:

I'm not expecting you to be perfect, I just expect you to try your best. That's not unreasonable is it?

BELLA/WRITER:

Oh, no, it's not unreasonable, you would never be unreasonable, that's the whole problem! What's wrong with you? Your mum just died!

(Throws down glasses.)

Why can't you be unreasonable? Why can't you stop thinking, and controlling and rationalising and suppressing and compartmentalising and explaining and coping and just

NOT cope? What would happen if you just didn't cope with something for once in your life? Is that really the worst thing you can imagine? Are you really more afraid of not coping with your parents dying than you are of your parents actually dying for fuck's sake? Oh, never mind if that person you love is gone forever, as long as you can cope with it impressively well, and people can tell you how strong you are, and how they admire you. Because that's what matters, is it? That's what really matters – whether people think you're a good person, a shining beacon of bravery and humanity. No matter that you've switched off your feelings so much that you can say 'I'll never hear my dad's voice again' without crumpling into a puddle on the floor. How can you be okay with that? How can you smile and make a play about it and be more concerned with the theatrical merit of the piece than with the fact that you've lost the people that mattered most in the world? The people that made you and loved you more than anyone else ever could? Why can't you cry?

Why, even as you re-live the deaths of your parents, the actual, real life death of your actual parents, live onstage, can you not produce tears?

Call yourself an actor?

You're barely a person.

(Pause. BELLA/WRITER/GUIDE looks at the audience. Sits.)

I'm sorry Mum. I'm sorry I didn't howl when you died. You deserve my grief as much as Pete did. You deserve more. It's overwhelming, the grieving you deserve. My rage at your pain furiously eats up every glimmer of hope and hate tenses my muscles and I can't breathe, I can't live like that, I can't, so I push it down, away, behind me, and I forget to grieve, I fail to honour you. But I love you, mum. I do. I love you. I love you. I love you.

(Pause. ASSISTANT gets out a flask and pours a cup of tea.)

EVA/ASSISTANT/ACTOR:

Cup of tea?

(BELLA/WRITER/GUIDE nods. Goes over to piano and sits. Drinks some tea, then nods to EVA/ASSISTANT/ACTOR, who says–)

STEP 17: FEEL BETTER

EVA/ASSISTANT/ACTOR:

Just remember, you're allowed to feel how you feel, and eventually you'll feel better.

(BELLA/WRITER/GUIDE holds up reverse of APPLAUSE sign, which reads: **THE END***.)*